M...

120th
anniversary
Berlitz

- A ☞ in the text denotes a highly recommended sight

- A complete A–Z of practical information starts on p.101

- Extensive mapping on cover flaps

Berlitz Publishing Company, Inc.

Princeton   Mexico City   Dublin   Eschborn   Singapore

Text: Martin Gostelow
Editor: Jane Middleton, Sarah Hudson
Photography: Martin Gostelow, Richard Boyle
Layout: Media Content Marketing, Inc.
Cartography: 🌐 Falk-Verlag, Munich

Thanks to Air Malta, the Malta National Tourism Organization, Connie Grech, Leslie Agius, Mario Falzon, Joseph Abela and Avis Malta for their invaluable help in the preparation of this guide.

Found an error we should know about? Our editor would be happy to hear from you, and a postcard would do. Although we make every effort to ensure the accuracy of all the information in this book, changes do occur.

ISBN 2-8315-6315-5
Revised 1997 – Second Printing May 1998

Printed in Switzerland by Weber SA, Bienne
029/805 RP

CONTENTS

MALTA

THE ISLANDS
AND THE PEOPLE

The strategic position of Malta, Gozo, and Comino (which together comprise the nation we know as Malta) has made these Mediterranean islands a crossroads of history and often a bone of contention. Less than 100 km (62 miles) south of Sicily and 350 km (220 miles) north of the deserts of Libya, they are now easily accessible to today's jet-age travellers. Reliable summers and warm seas make them a great place for a beach holiday, with the added attractions of dozens of sights and monuments from a fascinating past.

Approached by air or sea, Malta can look arid and austere, especially when baked by a midday sun. But as you get nearer, the landscape of the main island takes on a special beauty. The pastel colours of the rocks are networked with dry stone walls, trapping pockets of greenery. Here and there a surprisingly large or opulent church will stand out from an almost biblical village scene of flat-topped houses. In cobalt-blue harbours and narrow inlets, the multicoloured luzzu fishing boats bob alongside yachts, cruise ships, and mammoth oil tankers.

Once on the ground, you'll find a land full of contrasts. In winter, even the most barren-looking rock sparkles with tiny wild narcissus and crocuses. And when spring arrives the hills blaze with colour. Horse-drawn carts vie for road space with big new cars and middle-aged collectors' pieces from the fifties, lovingly kept going by ingenious mechanics. Drivers keep to the left in Malta, and if you were to judge only from that and the bright red post and telephone boxes, you could believe you were in England.

The port city of Valletta, the capital, is ringed by massive bastions built originally for defence. Their architecture is admired by visitors from all over the world—for one of Malta's biggest industries these days is tourism. For most of the year the islands bask in sunshine, and while in summer the temperature can soar, wherever you are the temptingly clear blue Mediterranean is never far away and always ready to refresh. Winter visitors have increased in number year by year, fleeing the cold of northern Europe and attracted by lower off-season prices.

The main island of Malta covers just 246 sq km (95 sq miles), one-sixth the size of Greater London, and you can travel around easily from place to place by car, bus, or taxi. Gozo is even smaller, at 67 sq km (26 sq miles). Reached only by boat or perhaps by helicopter, it stays just the way its inhabitants and visitors like it—a rural outpost. Between

Many 1950's cars are still going, thanks to loving owners and ingenious mechanics. Take a drive past sparkling wild crocuses (opposite page).

Malta and Gozo, tiny Comino is about 2.6 sq km (1 sq mile) in area, and has one hotel, a handful of permanent residents, and no cars.

The total population of the island nation is estimated to be about 375,000, of whom about one in fifteen lives on Gozo. The first inhabitants arrived in the islands during Neolithic times, around 7,000 years ago. Colonized by almost

every Mediterranean power from Phoenicians to the Knights of the Order of St. John, and latterly the British, the islands finally became an independent nation in 1964.

From these differing roots, the Maltese have emerged. Visitors are invariably impressed by the islanders, who are among the most polite and good-natured people in the world. They are proud but also fun-loving, and know how to laugh at themselves as well as with everyone else. Work gets done—even back-breaking toil if necessary—but it is not taken too seriously.

Everyone speaks the Maltese language, Malti (Maltese), which is much more akin to Arabic than anything else (the numbers sound almost exactly the same in both). The affiliation of Malti with Arabic surely represents a remarkable survival. It is nearly 900 years since Arab rule was ended by the Norman invasion from Sicily, and since then various occupying powers have used strong pressure to get the people to use their language, whether it be Spanish, French, Italian, or English. Not surprisingly, words from each of the above did get incorporated, but generally Malti seems inaccessible to foreigners (see also Language on pages 115-117).

English-speaking tourists have few problems making themselves understood on Malta, as English is taught in schools and almost all Maltese speak it well. Italian too is widely understood—not only because it was the official language of the knights, but also because of the proximity of Italy. Today, many of Italy's television channels that broadcast from Sicily are picked up by forests of tall antennae in Malta, and the young generation is growing up with Italian children's programmes, pop music, and sports.

> **Maltese is a fusion of two linguistic branches: Semitic (Arabic) and Romance. It is spoken by about 300,000 people.**

Malta became Christian after St. Paul was shipwrecked there in A.D. 60. Today, you can visit the cave where the apostle is believed to have spent that winter. Religion is taken seriously in Malta; there are magnificent churches, wayside chapels, and shrines everywhere. Each parish is fiercely proud of its church—here this means giving your church more expensive ornaments and decoration, or raising a great deal of money and building an ever bigger one.

The loud bangs you hear on weekdays probably come from the huge quarries where workers dig out the stone for the rapid building programme. But during weekends in summer other explosions mark a succession of religious festivities, or festi. Each town and village celebrates its saint's day with parades, brass bands, and fireworks. The churches bring out their precious relics and their best silver and damask hangings. Streets and squares are decorated with huge statues of saints and special lighting, and they are thronged with people.

Malta has produced many good artists, though some of the finest paintings you'll see in the cathedrals, churches, and museums were done by the Italian painters Michelangelo Caravaggio and Mattia Preti. The chances are, however, that the building housing them was the work of one of the brilliant Maltese architects, such as Gerolamo Cassar or Lorenzo Gafà. Their designs and the warm local stone add up to a special look, unique to Malta.

The stonecarvers who embellished Baroque palaces with statues have modern counterparts. Look out for the graceful and dynamic figures of the 20th-century sculptor Antonio Sciortino, which can be found in museums and other

Horse-drawn carriages wait to take you on a grand tour of the narrow streets of Mdina.

public places. And although the local artisans' work today can be repetitive, you'll still find beautiful and original designs in blown and moulded glass, silver filigree, lace, and pottery.

The Maltese islands are far from being entirely given over to leisure facilities and the production of souvenirs. Part of their attraction is the way life goes on largely unaffected by tourism. Even the resort areas are a major part of the local scene. Farming, fishing, light industry (brewing, printing, canning and textiles), and Valletta's colossal dry docks and other ship-repair facilities are big employers. Even so, there have often been hard times and not enough work—many Maltese have emigrated in large numbers to Australia, Canada, and the United States. Those emigrants who have prospered overseas have been able to realize a dream—to come home. All over Malta and Gozo you'll see houses with names like "Sydney," or "God Bless America."

The islands are full of fun and surprises round every corner: children playing with a pet goat; an old woman clicking her bobbins to produce spiderwebs of lace; a karrozzin (a real "surrey with a fringe on top"). There's mystery, too, as you wander through the prehistoric ruins of some of the oldest temples on earth at Ħaġar Qim (see page 68) or Ġgantija (see page 76). No one can fully explain the strange lost civilizations that built them.

Geometrical perfection is displayed in a fish trap fashioned by a Gozo craftsman.

You won't need anyone to help you enjoy the pleasures of the seashore, the little sandy beaches, and the myriad water sports. Whatever your interests—archaeological, artistic, religious, or sporting—you'll find something to satisfy you on Malta, with the prospect of time to relax by the pool or a well-deserved leisurely lunch after your exertions.

A BRIEF HISTORY

Often ruled but never truly dominated, the Maltese islands command a place in history to match their strategic location. Over the centuries, each nation with power and ambitions in the Mediterranean has eyed Malta covetously. Violence, intrigue, and courage mark the many battles fought for their possession. Malta has been called "a palimpsest of history"—meaning an original manuscript erased and written over many times.

Civilization dawned on the islands long before recorded history. Fishermen setting sail from Sicily were probably the first to spot the islands, and in about 5000 B.C. (for a comment on prehistoric dates, see page 64) the first settlers arrived. They were Stone Age farmers, who lived in caves and villages and made simple pottery. A religious cult of the dead evolved—or was introduced—and became highly organized, to judge by the quite complex architecture of the time.

You can visit many of the prehistoric sites. One extraordinary underground complex of cave-like tombs on Malta is at Paola (see page 69). Known as the Hypogeum, it was in use from about 3200 to 2500 B.C., towards the end of the Stone Age in the islands. Its elliptical-shaped rooms and passages served as a burial chamber, and perhaps also a temple. The basic architectural forms found here also appear in such enormous stone temples as Ġgantija on Gozo and Ħaġar Qim (hah-jahr-khEEM) on Malta.

Some of the most magnificent prehistoric buildings were the temples of the Tarxien period (about 3200 to 2500 B.C.), named after the place where several of them are located. These are a stunning feat of construction for a supposedly primitive society. After them, the building of temples came to a sudden end, possibly as a result of invasion, though other theories suggest a plague or the pressures of overpopulation.

A new wave of immigrants appears to have come from southern Italy. Known as the "Cemetery People," they used the Tarxien temples as a burial ground but left only fragmentary traces of their culture. Far more relics have survived from the era of their Bronze Age successors, who built fortified villages—including Borg in-Nadur (borj in nah-DOOR), where the defensive wall dating from 1500 B.C. is still visible.

Carthage and Rome

By the 9th century B.C., Phoenician sailors from the eastern Mediterranean had reached the Maltese islands. At about the same time, they established a colony at Carthage in North Africa that grew into a great trading republic, eclipsing the Phoenician cities of the east and dominating the whole region. Inscriptions, coins and tombs remain as a record of their control in Malta.

The Great Cart Track Mystery

Some of the stoniest ground found in Malta and Gozo is criss-crossed with prehistoric "cart tracks."

These ruts have been discovered near village sites and quarries, and although they are not always of the same width and probably had nothing to do with wheeled carts at all, they seem to have been made by vehicles of some kind. These vehicles were probably "slide carts," with two shafts attached to a draught animal and dragging two stones linked by a crossbar. The load of building material or produce would have been carried on the bar.

Among the best places to see cart tracks are near Dingli, the so-called "Clapham Junction" site (see page 56), and Ta' Ċenċ on Gozo (see page 78).

The megalithic temples of Tarxien lay buried for thousands of years until rediscovered in 1913.

Greek civilization was another strong influence. The Greeks do not seem to have settled on Malta, but they had colonies in nearby Sicily and there was frequent contact between the island cultures.

When a new power, Rome, began to expand southwards, a clash with Carthage was inevitable. During the three Punic Wars between these two powers, from 264 to 146 B.C., the Carthaginians were forced to give up their empire and were finally defeated. Malta was taken by a Roman expedition in 218 B.C. under the command of the consul Tiberius Sempronius.

The Carthaginians had built their capital up on the hilltop in the center of the island where Mdina now stands, and the

Romans took this over, fortifying it and building luxurious villas elsewhere in Malta. You can see the remains of a Roman house between Mdina and Rabat.

One of Malta's most important historical events occurred during the Romans' rule. In A.D. 60, St. Paul and St. Luke were shipwrecked on the island, somewhere in the area now known as St. Paul's Bay, while travelling from Caesarea to Rome as prisoners. St. Paul's preaching in Jerusalem and Caesarea had caused such an outcry among the religious leaders there that the Romans had arrested him, partly for his own safety. During the subsequent enquiry St. Paul claimed the right, as a Roman citizen, to appeal to Caesar for justice.

For a whole winter the men stayed in a cave at Mdina–Rabat, and St. Paul preached the gospel. His message and the miracles that were reported to have happened in

The fine, intricate mosaic floor from the Roman villa at Rabat, near the Mdina Gate.

his presence began the conversion of the islanders to Christianity. Even the Roman governor, Publius, became a convert and was eventually named the first Bishop of Malta. He was later martyred and canonized. Despite the presence of many other religious influences since then, including a period of Moslem rule, Malta has remained fundamentally Christian from St. Paul's time to the present day.

Arabs and Crusaders

As the Roman Empire went into decline, it was divided into western and eastern sections. Malta was allocated to the east, governed from Constantinople. In A.D. 870, the Arabs became the new rulers.

Although the Arabs tolerated Christianity, many islanders emigrated, and some remaining Maltese became Moslem. At that time the slave trade was big business, pursued by both Arabs and the Maltese. The victims were mainly Christians who were captured either at sea or in raids on neighbouring coasts.

Two centuries of Arab rule left an indelible impression on Malta and especially on the language (see page 9). Cotton and citrus fruits were grown and became the mainstay of the economy as Malta's trade expanded.

What's in a Name?

The origin of Malta's name has often been debated. The most plausible theories are that it is either a corruption of the Phoenician malat (meaning "safe harbour"), or that it comes from the Greek meli (the word for "honey"), a famous product of the islands in early times.

Gozo (or Ghawdex, pronounced "Ow-dehsh") is probably derived from the Greek gaudos, which in turn comes from the Phoenician for a small boat.

However, quarrels among the Arabs eventually weakened the islands' defences, and the Norman Count, Roger I of Sicily, son of Tancred de Hauteville, seized his chance. Roger had inherited lands in southern Italy and Sicily and wanted to improve his strategic position by controlling Malta. He came ashore at St. Paul's Bay in 1090, later taking Mdina and the rest of the islands, which became part of the Kingdom of Sicily.

The new ruler was fairly liberal, letting the islanders govern themselves with local councils. The Christian church was encouraged to expand and renew itself, although Moslems were tolerated. Malta became a key link in the line of communication during the Crusades, while passing first into the hands of the Swabians and then to Charles of Anjou, brother

The walled city of Mdina was the capital of Malta under Carthaginian, Roman, and Arab rule.

of the French king, Louis IX. The French stayed until they were ousted in 1283 by Peter III of Aragon.

Exploitation by overseas feudal lords, interested in the country mainly as a source of revenue, continued under joint Spanish–Sicilian control. The Maltese worked at commerce, farming, and slavetrading, as well as piracy, in order to earn the taxes demanded of them.

By the 15th century, local self-government had evolved into an administrative body called the Università. Weary with having to pay extortionate dues to foreign nobles, the Maltese people raised money to secure instead a direct rela-

The Knights of St. John

The story of the Order of the Hospital of St. John of Jerusalem (the Knights Hospitallers) begins in the 11th century, when several Italian merchants obtained permission from the Moslem caliph to set up a hospice in Jerusalem for Christian pilgrims. The calling of the brothers of the order was principally to care for the sick, but in time the emphasis shifted to a military role, that of fighting for the faith.

In 1187 the knights, driven from Jerusalem by Saladin, had to move to Acre and then on to Cyprus. They retreated further, to Rhodes, in 1308, and though the Turks also besieged that island several times, it wasn't until 1523 that the power of Suleiman the Magnificent forced the knights to surrender and move on yet again.

The knights took vows of poverty, chastity, and obedience. They were divided into three main grades: Knights of Justice (from noble families all over Europe, who wore the eight-pointed cross now known as the Maltese cross), Sergeants at Arms (who acted as both soldiers and nurses), and Chaplains (who worked in the hospitals and churches).

The knights were grouped in eight *langues,* or "tongues," three of them French (France being divided in the 13th century into France, Provence, and Auvergne). The other *langues* were Aragon, Castile, Italy, Germany, and England. After the Reformation the English *langue* ceased to exist, though a new joint *langue* of England and Bavaria was formed in 1784. Each *langue* was headed by a *pilier,* who had a set function: thus the *pilier* of Italy was Grand Admiral; the *pilier* of Provence was finance and ordnance manager; the *pilier* of France was head of the order's hospitals. Their head, the Grand Master, was elected for life and was subject only to the authority of the Pope.

As the years passed, the knights lapsed into careless and even dissolute ways. Corruption and internal dissension undermined the effectiveness and reputation of the order. Some of the original ideals of the Hospitallers are continued in the St. John Ambulance Association: the order itself, now based in Rome, does mainly charitable work.

tionship with Spain. In 1428, King Alfonso V declared Malta "reunited in perpetuity" to the crown, cutting out the land-lords. However, the islanders' problems were not over. There were repeated attacks by Turkish raiders and pirates from North Africa. By the 16th century, with Spain's attention now drawn to the New World, morale in Malta was low and the economy was in decline.

The Knights of St. John

At this time, Suleiman the Magnificent, Sultan of the Ottoman Turks, practically ruled the Mediterranean Sea. The Knights of the Order of St. John had long since been expelled from the Holy Land but had found a base on the island of Rhodes off the coast of Turkey. Now, after repeated attacks and a six-month siege in 1522, the Turks took Rhodes on New Year's Day 1523, and the knights were adrift again.

Philippe Villiers de l'Isle Adam, the courageous Grand Master of the Order, led his soldiers to Sicily and Italy. But finding a more permanent home for the knights was becoming a thorny problem.

After seven years of negotiations, the knights reluctantly agreed to take over Malta in exchange for the payment of one falcon a year (the famous "Maltese falcon," though not much to do with the film of the same name). In 1530, the grand master and his 4,000 men moved to the new base.

Naturally, the islanders were uneasy about these new-comers at first, but their rights were properly respected and many appreciated the presence of these powerful protectors. The knights set about building fortifications and living quarters in Birgu (later called Vittoriosa) and the neighbouring peninsula, Senglea. As the Grand Harbour area became the focus of activity, so the importance of the old capital, Mdina, was correspondingly reduced.

Grand Master Villiers de l'Isle Adam died in 1534 and was succeeded by several other grand masters. Then in 1557 the leadership passed to one whose name was to become famous in Malta's history, Jean Parisot de la Valette.

Soon after the knights arrived in Malta, the Turks began to attack them again, with an eye to taking the island because of its strategic position on Mediterranean sea routes. North African pirates, under the command of one Dragut, were another threat. They devastated the island of Gozo in 1546 and took thousands of Gozitans as slaves in 1551. When Dragut then joined forces with the Turks, the future for Christendom looked bleak.

The Great Siege

Suleiman the Magnificent decided the time was ripe for new Islamic victories, so he began an unprecedented buildup of

warships and troops. Word reached Grand Master de la Valette, and he sent out desperate appeals for help, but only a few volunteers came. On 19 May 1565, a Turkish fleet of 138 galleys disembarked an army of 38,000 at Marsaxlokk Bay. Among them were 4,000 fanatical janissaries, most converts to Islam, who were trained only to be warriors.

The invaders, commanded by Admiral Piali and Mustapha Pasha, were confident of victory. De la Valette had only his 600 knights, 9,000 other troops and eight galleys, but they conducted one of the most valiant defences

Fort St. Angelo, Vittoriosa, was the knights' command post during the Great Siege.

23

in history. It was punctuated by disasters. After holding out for 31 days, Fort St. Elmo was finally overrun when the last defenders were killed. The Turks tied the corpses of the knights to crosses and floated them in the Grand Harbour, to the horror of their watching comrades at Birgu.

Dragut the pirate also died in this battle, struck by a cannonball, thus depriving the attackers of one of their most determined leaders. The spot where he fell, on Marsamxett Harbour, is now known as Dragut Point.

De la Valette strengthened his defences at Senglea and Birgu, and linked the two by a bridge of boats so that reinforcements could be rushed from one to the other. The crisis was at hand and all of Christian Europe seemed to hold its breath—but still sent no help. When word reached England, Queen Elizabeth I ordered prayers to be said in all the churches of her realm.

Throughout the terrible summer of 1565, heat, disease, and dwindling food supplies plagued both sides as they battled on. The Maltese people fought and suffered along with the knights in fierce resistance.

Despite their superior numbers, their explosives, and their dedication, the Turks were slowly worn down. Arguments between their commanders did not help. In one assault on Senglea, the Turks lost 2,500 men. Though the knights' losses were fewer, they were more serious because their troops were irreplaceable, and strategic positions were abandoned one by one for lack of troops to hold them. At one critical point for the knights, even de la Valette himself (though he was 72) threw himself into the fray, inspiring his followers by his courage.

At last reinforcements for the besieged were mustered by the Sicilian viceroy, Garcia de Toledo, and on 7 September they landed at Mellieha Bay. The Turks were running out of supplies, leadership, and spirit: fooled into believing the fresh troops to be more numerous than they really were, they lifted the siege. The remnant of their forces sailed away; historians estimate that well over two-thirds of their numbers had been lost. There followed general rejoicing in Malta, though the main island was devastated.

In the aftermath, there was fierce debate about reconstruction and new fortifications, the cost of which was clearly beyond the knights' resources. Some even suggested moving yet again to another base, but the European powers now proved to be more generous with money than they had been with help during the siege. Plans were drawn up for a new city between the two long harbours, on the Sceberras peninsula on the northeast coast. The Order obtained the services of the Pope's own architect, Laparelli. The capital Valletta—named after the dauntless de la Valette (the double L results from the Italian version of his name)—was born .

At the beginning of the two centuries of the knights' rule that followed, Malta's trade prospered and there was a building boom. Laparelli was succeeded by the Maltese architect Gerolamo Cassar, who was responsible for much of the way Valletta looks today, with harmonious styles that blend early Baroque with classical elements.

By the 18th century, however, Mediterranean traders were feeling the effects of competition from the alternative route to the riches of the East, around the Cape of Good Hope, and from the new magnet of the Americas. With their old enemies the Ottoman Turks no longer a threat, the order too was declining into a dissolute middle age. The French Revolution of 1789, and the subsequent downfall of the aristocracy and the church in France, deprived the knights of much of their support—and most of their revenue.

Enter Napoleon

In 1798, with mastery of the Mediterranean his objective, Napoleon came to the same conclusion reached by many commanders before and since: Malta would be valuable to him, and it would pose a serious threat if it were to fall into the hands of his enemies. On 10 June he invaded the island, landing at Valletta, and presented the knights with an order: They must pack up and leave. Where others had failed,

The inland towns of Malta (below is Attard) seem to bask, half asleep, in the afternoon sun.

Napoleon succeeded. Grand Master von Hompesch gave in, and, after 268 years of residence, the world's most famous military order departed.

Napoleon started energetically promulgating new laws, but then he too left, only six days after the knights. Two years of French rule followed, in which the arrogant behaviour of the occupiers made them hated by both the Maltese and the Church. A popular insurrection began, and troops sent by the King of Naples joined the Maltese.

With Admiral Nelson patrolling the Mediterranean, the French position was hopeless, and they capitulated in 1800. In 1802 the Treaty of Amiens gave Malta back to the Order of St. John, but subsequent Maltese protests prevented the knights from returning.

Malta's value as a naval base now came to the attention of the British, who had just relinquished Menorca. Great Britain informally administered the islands for the remainder of the Napoleonic Wars. British possession was formally recognized in the Treaty of Paris in 1814, and again at the Congress of Vienna.

British Colony

In 1813—a year marked by a plague that killed off a fifth of Malta's inhabitants—Sir Thomas Maitland arrived as governor. Nicknamed "King Tom," he dismissed the traditional self-governing Università and introduced sweeping reforms to bring the legal system into line with the English one.With this degree of stability and improving health standards, the population grew considerably. New crops were introduced, including potatoes, all of which flourished. Water resources were well managed and more vineyards were planted. The building of bases for the Royal Navy gave a boost to employment and prosperity. The opening of the Suez Canal in 1869 increased Mediterranean shipping, and by 1880 Grand Harbour was a major port.

During the 19th century a succession of constitutions gave Malta varying degrees of autonomy. Local riots after World War 1 brought about real changes, codified in the new Constitution of 1921. The Maltese became responsible for their own internal affairs, while London retained control defence and foreign affairs and matters affecting the Empire.

The Second Great Siege

Malta was vital to the Allied cause during World War II. Not only could ships and aircraft based there block the deployment of Italy's navy, they could also attack Axis supply routes to the German and Italian forces operating from North Africa. When Italy entered the war in June 1940, its first move was to bomb Malta. During 1941 Italian and later German bombers and fighters, based on Sicily and mainland Italy, kept up almost incessant raids.

> **Maltese did not exist in writing until the turn of the century.**

As Rommel made his advance through Egypt in the spring of 1942, enemy air attacks increased, and in March and April the islands were hit with more than twice the weight of bombs that fell on London during any *year* of the war. That summer life came close to being unbearable on Malta, with people living in cellars and caves in conditions of near-starvation.

The war cabinet in London decided to take the huge risk of sending a major convoy carrying desperately needed supplies. This perilous operation was code-named *Pedestal.* In August 1942, 13 supply ships and a tanker made their way, with both naval and air cover, through the Strait of Gibraltar. In a succession of Italian air attacks on the convoy, several of its ships were sunk, and the tanker *Ohio*, with its precious oil, was badly damaged. However, four cargo ships reached Valletta and on 15 August, despite five days of fierce bombardment, the *Ohio* was towed into Grand Harbour to a reception of weeping and cheering crowds.

The price of freedom had been high. Thousands of men, women, and children had been killed or injured and thousands of homes destroyed. It was only fitting, concluded Churchill, that Malta be awarded Britain's highest honour for civilian courage—the George Cross. To this day it appears on the national flag.

Independence

After the war, Britain gave Malta financial assistance with plans for reconstruction, and a new constitution granted the islands self-government within the Commonwealth. Plans for the complete transfer of power met with difficulties in both Malta and the United Kingdom, but, on 21 September 1964, Malta became fully independent, with a Governor-General and a Parliament of 50 members (now 65).

British forces remained on some military bases, but they finally left on 1 April 1979. Their withdrawal brought an end not only to the friction between Britain and the local government, but also to financial aid from Britain. As a result, many Maltese who had depended on the British services for their livelihood found themselves unemployed.

There was some sadness on both sides at the parting of the ways. Maltese pride in independence did not lessen their goodwill towards British residents on Malta and Gozo and the thousands of Britons who spend their holidays there.

The years since independence have seen the government change hands between the evenly balanced Nationalist and Labour parties. Malta's announced aim to join the European Union will only boost the self-confidence of a free nation.

WHERE TO GO

In this chapter we start with Valletta and the suburbs, move on to Mdina and Rabat, then visit the southeast coast and the northwest. The special section on Malta's prehistoric temples gathers together the information on these ancient and mysterious cultures for handy reference. Finally, we give a complete summary of where to go on Gozo.

But first, the city that has been at the centre of Malta's turbulent history.

VALLETTA

"That splendid town, quite like a dream," wrote Sir Walter Scott. When you see Valletta, whether from the air, or from a boat, or even from land in the glow of the late afternoon sun, you'll agree with him. The light turns the city's bright stone bastions and buildings to gold, making it a place of enchantment that seems to float on an indigo sea.

Valletta came to be when Jean Parisot de la Valette, the Grand Master, saw the defensive possibilities of the Sceberras peninsula. His imagination was fired. The sharply hog-backed ridge with its two great natural harbours, Marsamxett (mahr-sahm-SHEHTT) on one side and the Grand Harbour on the other, was the perfect place to build a heavily fortified capital. So it was that in 1566, despite the enormous cost anticipated, work was begun by Francesco Laparelli, who had served as architect to Cosimo de' Medici and Pope Pius IV. Laparelli is said to have masterminded the entire city plan in a mere three

days, and two years later, when he left, Gerolamo Cassar (his Maltese assistant) took over and kept to the original conception.

The new city was constructed quickly but intelligently. Around the uniform grid-shaped street plan, a solid line of stone curtains and bastions was built, which made it virtually impregnable. Fresh water remained a problem until the

Contrasts abound in Grand Harbour: a traditional dghajsa and a supertanker in for repairs.

17th century, when Grand Master Alof de Wignacourt ordered the construction of an aqueduct from springs near Mdina. This new supply even allowed gardens to be added to the fortifications.

Valletta suffered merciless bombing during World War II, but it was a victorious and courageous Maltese people who wept with joy when the blockade was broken in 1942 (see page 29). They are proud of their city, and have kept its original charms intact.

Around the Old Town

The best way to visit Valletta is on foot. Driving is inadvisable, as the streets are narrow and many are closed to traffic. Sunset is a good time for a walk around the town, when the shadows are cooling the streets and you can fall into step with strollers out for the evening social hour known as the *passeggiata*.

Fortifications Galore

In the 16th century, any new city required fortifications of one kind or another. Valletta, Floriana, and their surrounding suburbs can boast enough bastions, curtains, forts, towers, cavaliers, ravelins, ramparts, trenches, ditches, walls, and other defensive structures to send any budding military engineer into ecstasy.

The typical zigzag bastion provided the most effective type of defence. The nearer the enemy approached the bastion, the easier it became for the defenders to fire on the attackers along the flanks. Defences were thus "strengthened" without a real increase in arms, ammunition, or men.

The best way to appreciate Valletta's fortifications (most of which date from 1566-1570) is to walk along the tops of them. To go round completely takes about two hours (allowing time for stopping to admire the views).

The Auberge de Castile et Léon, now the PM's office, was originally designed by Cassar.

From the roundabout bus terminal and Triton Fountain, a footbridge crosses the deep rock-cut defensive ditch. You pass through the City Gate—rebuilt in postwar style—and into Freedom Square, with an arcade and complex of shops on either side. Directly ahead is Republic Street, which is closed to motor traffic for most of the day. Parallel to it on the right is the second principal artery, Merchants Street. Both streets run on for 1.5 km (almost a mile) to Fort St. Elmo at the end of the peninsula.

Opposite City Gate you'll see the sad ruins of the classical old opera house built by E.M. Barry—a reminder of the bombing in World War II. To the right is Valletta's oldest church, the Baroque **Our Lady of Victory,** completed in 1567 as a commemoration of the Great Siege victory (the church's façade was remodelled in the 17th century). Next to the church stands one of the earliest houses built in the city, now restored after damage during the war. Opposite is the church of St.

Catherine of Italy, a domed structure originally designed by Gerolam Cassar, but renovated heavily over the years.

A few steps farther on is the **Auberge de Castile et Leon,** the most impressive of the *auberges,* now housing the office of the Prime Minister. (The *auberges,* or inns, are the buildings where the knights were accommodated. Each *langue* had its own *auberge.*) Unfortunately, all the public can see of the auberge is its stunning exterior.

Just beyond Castile Place are the **Upper Barrakka Gardens.** With these green shrubs,

A statue of Queen Victoria bespeaks 165 years of British rule in Malta.

bright hibiscus, and statues, the gardens were built in the 18th century as a pleasant retreat where the knights would stroll and hatch plots. Among the statues you'll see now are a group of children, *Les Gavroches,* by Antonio Sciortino, the Maltese sculptor; a monument to Lord Strickland, the Prime Minister from 1927 to 1930; a bust of Sir Winston Churchill; and the tomb of Sir Thomas Maitland, "King Tom," the peppery governor of Malta (and Corfu) from 1813 to 1824 (see page 27). Unfortunately the gardens are now a haunt for prostitutes.

From under the colonnade here there's a stunning **view** across Grand Harbour. On the far left guarding the harbour mouth is 17th-century Fort Ricasoli; directly ahead is Fort St.

Angelo (Grand Master de la Valette's headquarters in the Great Siege) at Vittoriosa; to the right is Dockyard Creek, where the knights had their boats repaired. The next promontory is Senglea (see page 47), behind which rises the town of Cospicua, built later when the defensive walls were extended by Grand Master Cotoner. Directly below you, on Lascaris Wharf, is the old Customs House, attractively built in Venetian style, and the War Rooms.

Return to Merchants Street and you'll see **Parisio Palace,** on the right, where Napoleon stayed for a few days in 1798. Now the Ministry of Foreign Affairs, the palace is a sober 18th-century building. The Auberge d'Italie, on the opposite side of the street, was built by Cassar in the 16th century, was later modified and is now the General Post Office.

Make your way from Merchants Street to **Republic Street** via Melita Street. This thoroughfare is a hive of activity, lined with all kinds of shops, cafés, and snack bars. The **Church of Santa Barbara** (between South Street and Melita Street) is unusual for its simple decoration and oval shape beneath a soaring dome. This church was used by the knights of the *langue* of Provence. Today the Catholic services here are held here in English, French, and German.

The **Auberge de Provence,** on your left as you head towards Fort St. Elmo, now houses the **National Museum of Archaeology** (for opening hours, see page 120). This *auberge,* founded in 1574, was designed by Cassar.

The museum's collection, begun in the 17th and 18th centuries and reorganized in the 20th century by the Maltese archaeologist Sir Themistocles Zammit, was brought here when the museum was inaugurated in 1958.

It's essential to see this collection for a better understanding of Malta's prehistoric sites. Among the fascinating objects here are the celebrated 13 centimeter (5 inch) long

"Sleeping Woman" statuette from the Hypogeum underground burial chambers, and the huge lower half of a "fat lady" transplanted from Tarxien, where she was being eroded by the elements. Stones showing the early "pitted" style of decoration or the later spiral form have been brought here from Ħaġar Qim, Tarxien, and other sites (and replaced there by replicas) for the same reason.

There are also artifacts from each of Malta's prehistoric periods—such as carbonized seeds and weapons, and a curious Tarxien plate engraved with bulls and goats. The shards of big bowls and vases from the Tarxien period have since been reassembled; from the number found, it is thought that breaking vessels may have been part of an ancient religious ritual.

Upstairs, the museum has some interesting Roman and Punic (Carthaginian) pottery and jewellery, and a *cippus* (small pillar) with inscriptions in both Phoenician and Greek that enabled scholars to find the key to the deciphering of Phoenician. Its twin was given to Louis XIV and is now in the Louvre in Paris.

If you turn again towards Fort St. Elmo after leaving the museum, you'll see **St. John's Square** and the Co-Cathedral just off to the right. A crafts centre is housed in a corner of the square, and the neighbouring section of Merchants Street becomes a delightful open-air market on weekday mornings (on Sundays it moves to St. James' Ditch).

St. John's Co-Cathedral (for opening hours, see page 120), the knights' own church, was built between 1577 and 1577 to the plans of Gerolamo Cassar. Considered to be the architect's masterpiece, it was raised to its cathedral status in 1816 by Pope Pius VII, sharing the distinction with Mdina Cathedral (hence the "Co-").

The building's rather plain façade does nothing to prepare you for an interior that reveals a staggering display of Baroque art. Sir Walter Scott wrote that he had never seen a more striking church nave. The barrel-vaulted space is 58 meters (190 feet) long, 20 meters (65 1/2 feet) high, and 35 meters (115 feet) wide, and flanked on both sides by **chapels,** most of which were assigned to the various *langues* of the knights and named after saints. Everywhere you look, this church is densely carved in high relief, gilded or richly painted with religious motifs.

To the right of the nave are the chapels of St. James, St. George, St. Sebastian, and the Blessed Sacrament. The Chapel of the Blessed Sacrament last has an extraordinary **screen** and **gates** in solid silver, which, legend has it, were cleverly concealed by being painted black when the French were on a pillaging spree during their occupation of 1798.

The vault of the church is decorated with oil-on-stone **paintings** by the 17th-century Calabrian artist Mattia Preti that tell the story of St. John the Baptist. They took five years (from 1662 to 1667) to complete.

The rich **high altar** (1681) presents an elaborate array of marble, silver plate, and lapis lazuli. The group behind the altar is of the Baptism of Christ, by Sicilian sculptor Giuseppe Mazzuoli.

The **crypt,** entered from the Chapel of Provence, may be viewed through its gate, and visited on request between 10:00 A.M. and noon; it contains the tombs of the first 12 grand masters of Malta.

Going back towards the main door you'll see on the right the chapels of St. Charles (or of the Holy Relics), St. Michael, St. Paul, St. Catherine (containing *St. Jerome* by Caravaggio), and the Chapel of the Magi. Most of the chapels have monuments that commemorate grand masters. In the sacristy are paintings by Stefano Pieri, Preti, and Antoine de Favray.

To reach the **oratory and museum,** take a door on the right facing the altar, first bay from the entrance. The oratory's main feature is the monumental painting by Caravaggio, *The Beheading of St. John,* which is widely considered to be the finest painting in Malta. The painting dramatically uses *chiaroscuro* and lively Baroque composition well suited to its violent theme.

Commissioned by the order to paint several works, the hot-tempered Caravaggio ended up assaulting one of the knights. The details of the story are unclear, but the artist left the island in disgrace in 1609. Back on Republic Street and continuing towards Fort St. Elmo, you'll come to Great Siege Square, with its powerful allegorical monument by Sciortino. Opposite are the new Law Courts, an imposing neoclassical building on the former site of the Auberge d'Auvergne, destroyed during World War II.

Republic Street widens into **Republic Square.** Most of the square is taken up by a spacious outdoor café, and it is lined with little shops under the shady arcades. At the back of the square is the **National Library,** once the library of the order. The library was constructed in the late 18th century to house the collection amassed by the knights and the archives of the order, which include documents dating back to the 11th century.

From Palace Square, which adjoins Republic Square, you can go through a big archway into the first courtyard of the **Grand Master's Palace,** now the seat of the House of Representatives and of the president of the Republic of Malta. In 1569 the nephew of Grand Master del Monte built here what was probably the first private house in Valletta. Later the

St John's Co-Cathedral is a stunning treasury of semi-precious stones and painted ceilings.

knights commissioned Cassar to enlarge it into a palace. Some parts of the palace house museums, and some of the state rooms are used for Presidential receptions and other national occasions.

You'll find two cool, green courtyards nestled in the palace grounds, one of them called Neptune Court after its statue. In the other, Prince Alfred's Court, look up to see the **clock** installed by Grand Master Pinto de Fonseca (1741–1773). If you are there, you can watch as the little figures strike a gong on the hour.

To visit the palace, take the staircase from Prince Alfred Court. In the council chamber, the meeting place of Malta's Parliaments from 1921 to 1976, you can sit on one of the heavy bench seats and admire the beautiful Gobelins **tapestries** given to the order by Grand Master Ramon Perellos in the early 18th century. Called *Les Tentures des Indes,* the tapestries depict all kinds of real and fanciful beasts and birds, with exotically clad Indians. The paintings above depict the knights' naval victories.

The Hospital of the Order

The splendid buildings and halls of the Mediterranean Conference Centre started as the hospital of the knights in 1574.

The knights took in anyone of any faith who was ill, and treated the sick as *seigneurs malades* (sick lords)—with respect and humility. The standard of medical treatment was high and the patients were given good food served on silver dishes. All the knights, from the youngest novices to the grand master, served the patients.

The hospital was taken over by the French when they occupied Malta, and later by the British. The buildings have been well restored after the damage they sustained during the war.

The grandest of the public rooms is the Hall of St. Michael and St. George, or the Throne Room, with a beamed ceiling and frieze by Matteo Perez d'Aleccio. This is where the Supreme Council of the Order of St. John used to meet. Scenes of the Great Siege fill the walls, and the carved gallery comes from the ship in which Villiers de l'Isle Adam sailed away from Rhodes in 1523.

The damask-curtained **Hall of Ambassadors,** or the Red Room, features heavy portraits of assorted monarchs: Louis XIV by De Troy, Louis XV by Van Loo, Catherine II of Russia by Levitsky.

The old **Armoury,** upstairs from Neptune Court, serves as the hall of the Maltese parliament. The holdings of the armoury, including the suit of mail worn by Jean de la Valette and a gold-inlaid ceremonial suit made for Grand Master Alof de Wignacourt, are now housed in the palace stables.

Leaving the palace by the Neptune Court archway, you'll see the Greek Catholic Church on Archbishop Street—unremarkable except for a 12th-century **icon,** called "Our Lady of Damascus," which was brought by the knights when they came to Malta in 1530: it was well restored in 1966. Just a few steps away is the **Gesù Church,** built between 1592 and 1600, richly ornate in Italian Baroque style.

Go down Merchants Street and you'll find yourself at the **Mediterranean Conference Centre.** The restoration of this former hospital is one of the finest achievements of independent Malta. It opened as the impressive international conference hall in 1979.

The centre has six well-equipped conference rooms as well as a huge theatre and the beautiful 16 meter (528 feet) long vaulted hall that served as the Great Ward in the old hospital. A must for any visitor coming to Malta for the first time is the 45-minute multiscreen documentary, *The Malta Expe-*

rience, shown at the centre several times a day. It's an excellent introduction to the history of the islands. Headphones carry the commentary in six languages.

Star-shaped **Fort St. Elmo,** so valiantly defended during the Great Siege—though ultimately lost—occupies the whole of the end of the peninsula. You can enter the main part only if you have permission from police headquarters—the fort is a police academy now. However, within the fort you can visit the **National War Museum,** reached by a separate entrance (for opening hours see page 120). It contains mostly World War II relics, including *Faith,* one of the four Gladiator biplanes that were Malta's air defence when Italy declared war in 1940. The jeep *Husky* was used by General Eisenhower and later by President Roosevelt during a visit. The George Cross, conferred on Malta and the Maltese in 1942 for their courage under bombardment, is the most treasured exhibit.

Other Places of Interest

If you head back towards City Gate, Fountain Street brings you to the beginning of Strait Street (also known as the Gut), a narrow lane that still has some of the bars and hangouts that once gave it a reputation among sailors for lowlife. It was also the only place where the knights were allowed to fight duels. A slightly longer walk that follows the fortifications starts along St. Sebastian Street, with the English Curtain wall on the right and the rather run-down Auberge of the Bavarian *langue* opposite.

St. Sebastian Street brings you to St. Sebastian Bastion, with its spectacular view of Marsamxett Harbour. If you turn up Archbishop Street—actually a flight of steps at this point—you'll reach Independence Square. The **Auberge d'Aragon** here was the first *auberge* built in Valletta (in the

16th century), though the Doric porch was added at a later date. The building of the neoclassical St. Paul's Anglican Cathedral opposite was entirely paid for by the Dowager Queen Adelaide after she visited Malta from 1838 to 1839. St. Paul's 60 meter (197 feet) high steeple makes a striking landmark, rivalled by the huge dome of **The Carmelite Church** nearby on Old Theatre Street, an enlarged replacement for the original dome bombed during the war.

The **Manoel Theatre,** built in 1731 under the rule of Grand Master Manoel de Vilhena, is a gem, and one of Europe's oldest theatres still in use. It has endured periods of decay over the years, becoming at one time a dosshouse (the homeless could sleep in the theatre's boxes for a penny a night) and then a cheap cinema. Now restored as Malta's National Theatre, its neat, oval shape with tiers of gilded and painted boxes makes a splendid setting for both plays and concerts. (Tours begin at the box office in Old Theatre Street; for times see page 120.)

Across the peninsula are several Baroque churches: St. Roque and St. Ursula (both in St. Ursula Street) and **St. Paul Shipwrecked** in St. Paul Street, an 18th-century church with an ornate 19th-century façade. Its treasures include a **statue of St. Paul** by Melchiorre Gafà, a wrist bone of the saint, and half of the column on which he was beheaded in Rome.

> A man born on St. Mary's Day (August 15) is said to become a successful jockey and make a name for himself in horse-racing.

The **National Museum of Fine Arts** is situated on South Street, which crosses Republic Street up near City Gate. The building is an imposing 18th-century palace, built around a sunny courtyard. In its former incarnation as Admiralty House, the palace served as the official residence of the commander-in-chief of the British Mediterranean Fleet—a post filled at one time or another by practically every famous British naval hero, as the list inside reminds you.

The collection includes paintings from various periods of the Flemish, Dutch, French, and Italian schools, notably some by Mattia Preti, who came to decorate St. John's Cathedral and stayed. There are also some fine works by the 20th-century Maltese sculptor Antonio Sciortino.

The exhibits in the basement evoke the knights' hospital mission, with apothecary vessels, vases, and the famous **silverware** used to serve the patients. Also look for the early models of fortifications.

Near City Gate (up to the right before you exit) are **Hastings Gardens,** named after the Marquess of Hastings, who was Governor of Malta from 1824 to 1826 and whose funerary statue stands here. From here there is a splendid **view** of the surrounding area. You can see Marsamxett Harbour, Msida and Lazzaretto creeks, Manoel Island, and Dragut Point. Floriana and St. Publius Church are below you and Independence Arena is off to the left.

The mountainous **bastions** of St. Michael and St. Andrew built up here after the Great Siege are an impressive 18 to 21 meters (59 to 69 feet) thick. Walking back to City Gate, before taking a staircase down, you'll cross the fortifications of St. James' Cavalier and St. John's Cavalier (where the knights now have their Embassy in Malta).

Steps next to the tourist information office at City Gate, lead down into the great "ditch" that protected Valletta from landward attack. If you make the descent you'll see the lower-level bridge that once carried Malta's short and only railway, which went from Valletta only as far as the city of Mdina until it closed in 1931. The station here is now an underground car park.

In Lascaris Bastion, along the bottom of the ditch, the **War Rooms** have been preserved, complete with uniformed models. (For its opening hours, see page 120.)

AROUND VALLETTA

Floriana

Any approach to Valletta by land inevitably goes through the spacious Floriana area south of Valletta on the peninsula. Floriana is named after Paolo Floriani, the Italian military engineer who recommended that Valletta be protected by outer fortresses on the land approach. Here you'll drive under or beside the twin arches of **Portes des Bombes,** one built in the 18th century, another added later, in matching style, of course, by the British. On St. Anne Street are the British High Commission and the U.S. Embassy.

Vittoriosa, Senglea, Cospicua

Just across Grand Harbour east of Valletta are "the three cities"—the outlying areas of Vittoriosa, Senglea, and Cospicua. You can reach these areas by bus from City Gate, by car via Marsa or, if one is operating, by *dgħajsa* (water taxi) from Lascaris Wharf.

In **Vittoriosa,** still known as Birgu to the Maltese, the main street, Via Il-Mina L-Kbira, carries on down from the main gate to Vittoriosa Square. Halfway along you'll come to the former Inquisitor's Palace, a gloomy warren now partly turned into a folk museum. Just to the east of the square in Majjistral (or Mistral) Street is the pretty façade of the **Auberge d'Angleterre.** The diminutive church below the square is the Oratory of St. Joseph. An interesting museum here displays a variety of exhibits connected with Vittoriosa, including a sword and hat belonging to Jean de la Valette.

The **Church of St. Lawrence,** towards the waterfront, was originally the knights' Conventual Church before the move to Valletta. Rebuilt by Lorenzo Gafà in the late 1600s, it is richly decorated inside, with paintings and pink marble columns. Outside, a plaque records the death of Sir Nicholas Upton, who fell defending Malta from the Turks in 1551. Another plaque commemorates the people who died in a World War II bombing, when the church's dome was completely destroyed.

Below the church is the Freedom Monument, unveiled on 31 March 1979, when the British Navy finally departed; it shows a British sailor shaking hands with a Maltese dockworker. The bakery of the Royal Navy was the first of the buildings along the waterfront. Now, the bakery and adjacent buildings house the Maritime Museum.

The site of **Fort St. Angelo** had already been built on in Phoenician times with, it is thought, a temple to Astarte, fol-

The Harbour by Boat

The two-hour boat tours leaving from Sliema provide an excellent way to enjoy a sea view of Valletta and environs. Various companies run the trips several times daily, and competition keeps prices down. As you pass container ships and cruise ships, a guide points out the sights—such as the place where the knights put a huge chain across the harbour from St. Angelo to Senglea to keep the Turks out, and plus the forts and the docks.

In one of the "creeks", huge tankers are repaired. In another you'll see a dry-dock project built with the help of the People's Republic of China; the 29 meter (95 foot) tall crane here is one of the world's largest, capable of lifting 150 tons. There are more romantic vistas to be had, however, especially of the majestic bastions, spires, and domes of Valletta itself.

lowed by a Greek temple to Hera and a Roman one to Juno. During the Great Siege the knights moored their galleys in the moat (now partly filled in) between the fort and the town, when St. Angelo was their command post. The fort was also the Royal Navy's headquarters during World War II, and it held up well, considering how often it was bombed.

Senglea and Cospicua were also heavily blitzed, and since the war they have been rebuilt in modern style as residential areas. **Senglea,** also called L'Isla, was named after the

Carved eyes and ears mark out a lookout post on the walls at Senglea.

grand master who fortified it before the Great Siege, Claude de la Sengle. Make your way to the little garden at Isola Point, where a lookout tower is aptly sculpted with an eye and an ear.

Cospicua (also known as Bormla), is ringed by the formidable multiple walls of the **Cotonera lines,** named after the 17th-century Grand Master Cotoner.

Sliema and St. Julian's Bay

West of Valletta across Marsamxett Harbour, these are the liveliest spots in Malta for hotels, nightlife, and shopping.

Sliema, a thriving suburb of 25,000 people, is a lot larger than Valletta. It's about a 5 km (3 mile) journey from Floriana to Sliema's Strand, passing by or through Pieta, Msida, and Ta' Xbiex, where yachts line the quayside.

Sliema has grown fast in recent years and its general appearance is undistinguished, yet it has good shops, restaurants, and a range of hotels. The harbour shore is a concrete promenade, but the rocky northeast coast, facing the open sea, has suitable flat spots for swimming. The peninsula facing Valletta was once a big military base, now being converted to housing and leisure facilities. At Dragut Point, the eponymous pirate was killed during the bombardment of St. Elmo in 1565.

After St. Julian's Point, with its fortified tower (now a café) you reach Balluta Bay, and then **St. Julian's Bay,** an old fishing village that has sprouted bars and restaurants. Between here and St. George's Bay are luxury hotels, discos, and the casino. The entire area swarms with bathers on summer weekends.

INLAND TO MDINA AND RABAT

Mdina (im-DEE-nah) is about 12 km (7 1/2 miles) west-southwest from Valletta, through busy Hamrun, an industrial suburb. The road passes the **aqueduct,** built in the 17th century by Grand Master Wignacourt to bring water to Valletta. Off to the right from Attard, the **San Anton Gardens** make a refreshing, shady retreat, with subtropical trees and flowers, and some giant evergreens—possibly descendants of the islands' lusher past when plenty of rain and greenery supported abundant wildlife. At the opposite end of the gardens is the official residence of Malta's president; it was built as a summer palace in the 17th century by Grand Master Antoine de Paule.

Farther along the road, also branching off to the right, is Ta' Qali, a former airfield now converted into a crafts village (see page 88).

Mdina

This historic citadel and the medieval city that grew up around it, constitute one of Malta's most beautiful spots. The promontory may have been inhabited since the Bronze Age, and there were certainly Punic and Roman settlements here.

The Romans called the promontory *Melita* (honey); St. Publius, the Roman governor (converted by St. Paul and later to become first Bishop of Malta) lived here. When the Arabs fortified the promontory in the 9th century they renamed it *Mdina* (the walled city) and separated it from its "suburb," Rabat (which means "city" in Arabic).

Also known as *Città Notabile*, Mdina was the first capital of Malta and later the Bishop's See and seat of the Università, the government advisory body. Count Roger of Normandy was greeted here as the island's liberator from the Arabs in 1090. When the knights decided that Valletta should become the capital, Mdina became *Città Vecchia* ("old city").

Now it is often called "the silent city," intriguing and secretive with narrow, practically deserted streets. Several of Malta's aristocratic old families still live here—very discreetly in enclosed palaces.

Two main gates (both dated 1724) lead into Mdina. On the left is Greeks' Gate. However, it is better to take the bridge across the moat from Howard Gardens and enter the town through **Mdina Gate** (the outline of an earlier gate is to the right of it). Vilhena Palace, just inside the gate, is named after the grand master who had it built in the 18th century. It currently houses the quaint Museum of Natural History, which has interesting exhibits on the geology of Malta. You can visit the Mdina dungeons below.

Villegaignon Street is the main thoroughfare of Mdina, running all the way through town to the wall on the opposite side of the city.

To the right is the Nunnery of St. Benedict, a blank-walled building to which men (except priests) are not admitted. The two churches of St. Peter's and St. Agatha's are nearby, and on the left you'll see **Casa Inguanez,** the palace home of Malta's oldest titled family. Typically, the main entrance is in a side street.

The striking **cathedral** (the seat of the bishopric and "co-cathedral" with St. John's in Valletta) is an outstanding Baroque work on an island rich in Baroque art. Fronted by a pair of cannons, flanked by its two bell towers, it has three doorways with two different types of pilasters (Corinthian below and composite above), making an admirable façade when it is seen from the square. Redesigned and reconstructed by Lorenzo Gafà between 1697 and 1702, it is considered to be his masterwork.

Intriguing, secretive, and shadowy—all these words describe Mdina.

The interior, under an impressive dome, is well proportioned, yet very rich, and the marble mosaic floor covers the tombs of bishops and notables.

Notice that the heavy wooden **doors** through the vestry are carved with snakes and other motifs. *The Shipwreck of St. Paul,* a **painting** by Mattia Preti, is in the apse, and to the left of the apse you'll find a silver **processional cross,** brought to Malta (according to tradition) from Rhodes by the knights.

The Mdina Gate leads to the quiet city, where the streets stay mysteriously shady and cool.

Just outside the Cathedral, a former seminary houses the **Cathedral Museum,** with a fine **coin collection** that will thrill any numismatist. Displayed in mirrored cases, the collection takes you from Carthage all the way to modern Europe.

Upstairs is a collection of paintings (Sicilian, Flemish, and Spanish, from the 16th to the 18th centuries), superb Dürer woodcuts, and delightful engravings by Rembrandt,

The dome of Mdina's St Paul's Cathedral,
built three centuries ago by Maltese architect Lorenzo
Gafà, will impress everyone.

Piranesi, Van Dyck, and Goya. Some beautiful illuminated choirbooks date from as early as the 11th century.

Just off the square in Villegaignon Street is the **Palazzo Santa Sophia,** whose ground floor is reputedly the oldest in Mdina, with a typical Maltese feature—a "stringcourse" of triangular corbels with balls attached to them. The upper floor was finished 600 years later—to the original plan!

The next big building on the left is the **Carmelite Church.** Its bells played an important part in the 1798 revolt against the French, who wanted to sell valuable tapestries belonging to the church. In a now legendary incident a young boy attacked the French Commandant Masson, inciting a riot. The bells of the church were rung to call people from the neighbouring countryside. After a good deal of brawling, an enraged Maltese crowd threw Masson to his death from a balcony. This incident was one of the first actions of the rebellion that lasted until the French were ousted in 1800.

Near the end of Villegaignon Street on the right is the **Norman House,** or the Palazzo Falzon. The lower, and earliest, part of the house is a defensive façade built in the 14th and 15th centuries, with only slits for windows. The later and upper section has attractive double-arched windows.

At the end of the street you'll come to a large **bastion** with a magnificent **view,** extending to Mosta with its great dome and all the way to the spires of Valletta in the east. Head for Greeks' Gate, diverting along any of the narrow alleys on the way, and you'll see how the city was designed to create cool shade, as well as for defensive purposes. Even if enemies penetrated the walls, they could be pelted with missiles from the rooftops, or cut off in dead-end streets.

At **Greeks' Gate,** you can see blocks of Roman masonry in the lower wall, and the outline of an Arab archway, illustrating the long history of this little jewel of a city.

Rabat

Rabat is Mdina's twin city. The **Roman villa and museum,** near the gates of Mdina, is worth visiting. This small, columned building made of pinkish stone, and garlanded with rhododendrons, has been built over the mosaic floors and outline walls of the Roman original. Inside, you can see pottery from Carthaginian and Roman tombs as well as some superb Roman glass.

Downstairs in the atrium you'll find the fine mosaics, some made of especially tiny tesserae, which account for the delicate detail of the pictures. The adjoining Arab cemetery fortunately managed to just miss the mosaics when its graves were dug.

St. Augustine's Church, found on St. Augustine Street, was built by Gerolamo Cassar two years before the cathedral in Valletta. The latter is foreshadowed by the former, especially by its massive barrel-vaulted interior.

In the heart of Rabat, on Parish Square, is the 17th-century **St. Paul's Church.** Next to the church (on the left, downstairs) is the entrance to **St. Paul's Grotto,** where the saint supposedly took shelter when he was in Malta. Legend has it that no matter how much stone was extracted from the cave, by some miracle it always grew back.

The **catacombs** west of Rabat (St. Paul's and St. Agatha's; signs point the way) are cool mazes of galleries and passageways. Their extent suggests that a large Christian community lived in the area in the 4th and 5th centuries. The circular stone platforms are thought to have been tables for funeral feasts where guests reclined in the Roman style, and some of the chambers seem to have been used for prayer meetings. St. Agatha's catacombs show traces of frescoes depicting saints, doves, and shell designs.

Verdala, Buskett, Dingli

Verdala Castle lies just east off the road from Rabat to Buskett, a few minutes from Rabat. (Note the castle is not open to visitors.) Once the summer residence of Grand Masters and Governors, it is now an occasional retreat for the President and guests. Cassar built this square castle surrounded by a moat and pine groves in 1586 for the Grand Master de Verdalle, Cardinal Verdala. It has a magnificent elliptical **staircase** and a superb view from the roof.

At the **Buskett** or *Boschetto* (meaning "little wood"), one of the island's greenest spots, the knights raised their falcons for hunting. On 28 and 29 June, Malta's folklore festival is held here. About a mile away you come to Girgenti, the summer palace of the Inquisitor, a good place for him to relax from his weighty duties. (It is not open to visitors.)

The nearby **Dingli Cliffs** drop 250 meters (820 feet) to the sea, providing a dizzying view. The islet in the distance is Filfla, made even smaller by the British who used it for bombing practice.

A painting in Verdala Castle depicts the investiture of the man who built it, Cardinal Verdala.

Between the Buskett Gardens and the cliffs, signs to "Clapham Junction" (a joke reference to the busiest London train station) direct you to one of the best areas to see prehistoric **"cart tracks"** (see page 14). A broad rocky slope is grooved in rectangles where great stones were quarried, and deep, curving double tracks lead down the hill. The ruts were etched by some kind of sled on which the stones were dragged away.

SOUTHEAST COAST

Ghar Lapsi is a mere cluster of buildings under the cliffs, but it is one of the few ways down to the sea near here, so the tiny beach is a local favourite. Farther east, by the road to Żurrieq,

Cart tracks were made by dragging sleds full of stones.

is Malta's **Blue Grotto**— not as large as Capri's, nor as crowded. The approach road offers some spectacular views and leads to a small car park, where you'll find boatmen in colourful water taxis ready to shuttle you around the point and into the limestone caves. Try to go in the morning before 10 o'clock, when sunlight slants into the caves to reflect off the white sandy bottom. In some places your hand will glow turquoise blue if you drag it in the water.

The 25-minute excursion takes in several caves, where the limestone is tinted pink, mauve, and orange by coral and miner-

Malta's Blue Grotto is as beautiful as the one in Capri— but much less crowded.

als, especially in one called "Reflection Cave." In the best light, the Blue Grotto itself is a luminous, pure blue, and a square natural "window" in the rock gives the effect of a fluorescent lamp.

While you're in the area, you can visit the twin temple sites of Ħaġar Qim and Mnajdra, which are close at hand on the cliff top (see pages 13 and 68).

Marsaxlokk (Mahr-sash-LOKK), on an eastern arm of Marsaxlokk Bay, is the largest fishing village in Malta, colourful and peaceful, with bobbing *luzzu* boats, fisher-

After being shipwrecked near Malta in A.D. 60, St. Paul came ashore on an island in St. Paul's Bay.

men mending their nets, and a good choice of seafood restaurants around the harbour. Also in this area is the pre-historic site of Għar Dalam (see page 64) and Pretty Bay, once a favourite local holiday haunt, though industry and modern installations have made it less worthy of its name.

Dragut the pirate landed in Marsaxlokk in 1565, and in the 17th century several defensive towers were built. The towers didn't deter Napoleon, whose troops disembarked here in 1798. In more modern times the bay was a seaplane base.

A small road running down to **Delimara Point** takes you

past Tas-Silġ Chapel, where there is a Carmelite Monastery, and the site of a Punic-Roman temple. You can swim from the rocks at Peter's Pool, and nearby St. Thomas Bay is shallow, sandy, and popular with windsurfers. Between the two, at Xrobb Il-Għagin, are some vestiges of a Neolithic temple.

Marsaskala, at the head of its own narrow bay, is like a smaller Marsaxlokk, complete with pastel houses and colourful fishing boats. Rapid building in recent years has

The immense dome of Mosta's church is justly proud of its title as one of the world's biggest.

lined the inlet with apartments and villas and, where the inlet meets the sea, one of Malta's largest hotels.

THE NORTHWEST

Although relatively fertile, this part of Malta was once difficult to defend, and so was under-populated. It is still more rural than other parts of the island, and its sandy beaches are now a big attraction.

As you're heading this way, you will hardly miss one of the island's outstanding landmarks, the **dome** of the parish church in the busy little town of **Mosta.** St. Mary's was built with local money and by voluntary labour between 1833 and 1860 to the designs of the architect Giorgio de Vassé, and the inhabitants are justly proud of it.

The enormous dome, whose 37 meter (121 1/2 foot) diameter makes it one of the largest in the world, was constructed without the use of scaffolding. Behind a classical façade, the impression one has on entering the church is, not surprisingly, of being inside a giant dome, and the geometrical marble floor heightens the effect. A bomb fell through the dome on 9 April 1942, sliding across the floor without exploding—a miracle for the people present. A replica of the bomb stands in the sacristy on the left.

Nearby **St. Andrew's,** once a huge army base, has now been converted into civilian housing and holiday facilities. The road runs alongside the coast again at Bahar ic-Cag-ħaq, where there is a water slide park. After passing several headlands and old towers, you arrive at **Salina Bay,** with a small

The sirocco is a strong wind blowing from North Africa between May and September. It brings dust, heat and humidity, and it slows life down considerably on the southern parts of the islands.

playground, salt pans, and reedbeds. Farther round the bay at **Qawra** (KhOW-rah; remember, the "Q" is almost silent), big resort hotels, and beach clubs offer plenty of water sports facilities.

Next, by rounding Qawra Point (where the knights' fort is now a restaurant) or by cutting across the peninsula, you will come to **St. Paul's Bay.** On its south side, **Buġibba** (Boo-JIB-ba) village and the town of San Pawl il-Bahar have grown together into a major holiday resort, with water sports and swimming from the rocks or small sandy beaches. Hotels, apartments, restaurants, bars, and discos have sprung up, but traditional life continues, too, in the old parts of town and at the fishing harbour.

St. Paul came ashore near here after he was shipwrecked in A.D. 60. The legend goes that it was on the larger of the two islands you can see over the water. Għajn Razul ("apostle's fountain") is said to be where he struck a rock, which miraculously brought forth water.

Mistra Bay is an inlet within St. Paul's Bay, on the opposite shore from the town and harbour. Reached by a road through the rural landscape and reedbeds of Kalkara Ravine, it has the advantage of a sandy, although sometimes weed-covered, beach.

For some really fine views, walk the rocky tracks round the headland facing St. Paul's Islands. Another way to enjoy the scenery is to drive up the hill to Selmun Palace, once a knights' redoubt, now a hotel.

Mellieħa Bay, just under Marfa Ridge (the "tail" of fish-shaped Malta), is the biggest stretch of sandy beach in the islands, and likely to be crowded in the high season. Perched on the commanding spur of Mellieħa Ridge, the town of **Mellieħa** itself has a superb view of Marfa Ridge and Comino, with Gozo stretching beyond. The stone church, standing like a reddish fortress on the promontory, dates from the 19th century, but nestling within is a chapel from the early Middle Ages, now a site of pilgrimage. A small chapel in a grotto next to the church contains a fresco of the Virgin that is attributed to St. Luke.

To drive or walk along **Marfa Ridge** is almost like flying, the views in all directions are so spectacular. The knights' **Red Tower** (1649) is the most prominent of the defence posts from various eras that dot the ridge. On the ridge's northern shore, you'll find stretches of sandy beach and hotels at Armier, Ramla, and Paradise Bays. Ċirkewwa is the landing stage where you can take the car ferry for the 20-minute crossing to Gozo.

Rocky and beautiful **Anchor Bay,** across the narrow neck of land from Mellieħa Bay, was so named because its shores were once littered with anchors. Children will be thrilled to discover the engagingly ramshackle **Popeye Village,** constructed there as the set for the film *Popeye* and retained as a tourist attraction. A small admission fee is charged, but you can then use the beach for as long as you like.

Golden Bay *(Ramla Tal-Mixquqa),* on the western shore of the island, is a broad crescent of sand that is not always pristinely clean but has a good selection of cafés and a big tourist complex on the hillside just above.

The much smaller Għajn Tuffieħa Bay, just next door, is reached via a long staircase (though more and more cars seem to be illegally following dirt tracks down to the beach). The beach here attracts (and can accommodate) fewer swimmers than Golden Bay. Inland to the south, you'll find the interesting remains of a Roman bathhouse. Charming **Ġnejna Bay,** with its colourful boathouses cut into the cliffs, has a sheltered, calm sandy beach.

THE PREHISTORIC SITES

Malta's prehistory is impressive and enigmatic. Settlement began with the arrival of agricultural immigrants who came from Sicily around the year 5000 B.C. Further waves of immigrants followed; the corresponding phases of development have been classified and given names that you'll encounter both at prehistoric sites and in museums.

All prehistoric dates must be regarded as approximate. The dates quoted here agree with the latest available research, including the technique of dendrochronology (or tree-ring dating), which gives dates that are substantially earlier than dates obtained from carbon-14 testing.

The different stages of Maltese prehistoric civilization have been named after the important sites associated with them, such as: the **Ghar Dalam** (ahr DAH-lam) period, lasting up to about 4500 B.C.; the **Skorba** period (4500 to 4100 B.C.); the **Zebbuġ** period (3900 B.C.); the **Mġarr** period (3700 B.C.); and the **Ġgantija** (J'GAHN-tee-yah) period (3600 to 3000 B.C.).

Outstanding among the Ġgantija sites are the temples at Ġgantija on Gozo (see page 76), Ħaġar Qim, and an early temple at Tarxien. The Hal Saflieni Hypogeum is a remarkable complex possibly dating back to 3300 B.C. and through the Tarxien period (around 3200 to 2500 B.C.), which left impressive temples at Tarxien, Mnajdra, Skorba, and Borġ in-Nadur.

Then, around 2500 B.C., temple-building inexplicably came to a sudden end. Drought and starvation, emigration, religious hysteria, and mass suicide have all been suggested as possible reasons.

The next group of immigrants used Tarxien as a cemetery from about 2500 to 1500 B.C.—they're called the **Cemetery People.** Around 1500 B.C., the **Borġ in-Nadur** (Bronze Age)

*At Ħaġar Qim on the south coast,
the megalithic temples go back over 5,000 years.*

period began with the last group of migrants to arrive—until the Phoenicians came about 800 B.C.

Few hard facts are known about the religion practised by the temple-builders. Phallic symbols, triangles, the huge, fat and skirted figure at Tarxien (the original is in the Valletta National Museum), and various smaller versions would seem to suggest a fertility cult.

The temples' curved outer walls were usually made of hard coralline limestone with faces or edges of blocks alternately projecting. Then came a packing of rubble and the inner walls, usually of globigerina limestone. Doorways and passages were erected on the trilithon principle—resembling posts and lintel.

Most temples were built in lobes or apses around a central court or passage. Common features included altars, possible "oracle chambers" and hollowed stones, perhaps used for collecting libations of blood from sacrificial animals. There was usually also a massive, concave front wall with an impressive entrance. Early temple interiors and altars had a pitted decoration and later there were carvings, which must have been done with stone, since no corresponding metal tools have been found.

Sophisticated metal-working techniques came to the islands during the Bronze Age, but the new immigrants produced nothing comparable to the earlier achievements, many of which pre-date other ancient wonders such as the Great Pyramid and Stonehenge. Maltese construction techniques are considered unique: it seems the builders invented everything themselves.

The following are some of the more interesting temples and caves to be visited. Go early in the morning if you want to avoid crowds (and heat) and go with a qualified guide if you don't want to miss the subtler details.

Għar Dalam is an important cave site about 10 km (6 miles) from Valletta. The small museum here shows the types

Prehistoric Economics

How were the tombs and temples of ancient Malta built and financed? The evidence suggests that the islanders lived peaceably together without much trouble from outsiders, and agriculture provided for the needs of the quite small population.

A tribal system with tithes paid to the chief would have made possible a structured society, able to pay priests and artisans, as well as providing organized labour to construct temples.

The people imported flint and obsidian to be used as tools, for these were not available locally. How they paid for imports is still unknown, though the medium of exchange may have been something perishable, but perhaps textiles or possibly even elaborate temple robes.

of animals that existed on Malta in the Pleistocene era. Exhibits include the fossilized remains of hippopotami and dwarf elephants. At one time the sea covered Malta, and as it receded probably left a land bridge to Sicily, by which the large animals crossed. As the climate grew drier and food became scarcer, the number of animals gradually dwindled, and dwarf varieties developed.

Uncovered from the late 19th century on, the natural cave intercepts a *wied*, or ravine, carved out of the hill by rushing water. Layers of detritus, including bones of wild animals, were washed down the ravine and into the cave. Human bones and carbonized grains found in upper layers show that the cave was inhabited in Neolithic times and that these earliest settlers were agricultural people. The cave is cool and restful, but there's not much to see aside from a few stalactites and stalagmites.

Less than a mile away, on the way to St. George's Bay, is **Borġ in-Nadur,** a village that was fortified around 1500 B.C., with some remaining ruins of houses and "cart-tracks" (see page 14) nearby. The strong defensive wall includes stones from earlier temples.

Skorba at Żebbiegħ is the oldest dwelling site in Malta, with a wall built before 4000 B.C., the remains of farmers' and herdsmen's huts, and two megalithic temples.

Ħaġar Qim and Mnajdra, about 13 km (8 miles) from Valletta, can be reached via Żurrieq or Siggiewi. The site of **Ħaġar Qim** is spectacular—high above the sea, with a view of Filfla island. You'll see the typical concave façade of the main temple and a complex series of rooms. Unusually, this temple is almost entirely built of the softer globigerina limestone, so it is eroded and weathered.

Interesting details include tethering loops for animals in the stone near the entrance, various "mushroom" or "tea-

Multiple stone doorways of a temple at Mnajdra, near Ħaġar Qim.

table" altars in the second court, and other altars with the early pitted decoration. A number of the famous "fat lady" figures—skirted cult figures with piano legs—were found in this temple and are now in the National Museum of Archaeology in Valletta (see page 35).

Mnajdra is a five-minute walk down a stone causeway towards the sea, in an even more beautiful setting. The temples here are contemporary with Ħaġar Qim, and the two sites have many features in common. But at Mnajdra, the stone is particularly subtly worked and curved. For an overview, climb a short way up the hill behind the site—in fact, you will have to limit your visit to this view, since the temple has been closed to the public for safety reasons and to thwart vandalism.

The **Hal Saflieni Hypogeum** (a Greek word meaning "underground") is in **Paola,** a southern suburb of Valletta. This eerie labyrinth, carved from soft limestone, is vast and overwhelming. It was hollowed out on three different levels, the deepest plunging to a depth of 12 meters (39 feet), and was discovered by accident when workers were digging cisterns for new houses in 1902. Professionally explored by archaeologist Sir Themistocles Zammit, it is one of Europe's

Filfla island lies just offshore from the ruins at Mnajdra and Ħaġar Qim.

most fascinating prehistoric sites and has recently been re-opened to the public after a restoration of visitors' facilities.

You descend by a modern spiral staircase into near-darkness. The first level would seem to be the oldest and cut the roughest (around 3300 B.C.). The two lower levels were made around the time of the Tarxien Temples (3200 to 2500 B.C.) and were carved out with increasing care and sophistication. The middle level has imitation corbelling, and carvings of doors and niches that cleverly copy the features of the above-ground temples. The Oracle Chamber has a hollow where men (and only men, it seems) can make an odd echo effect. The "sleeping lady" statuette (now in the National Museum) was found in the Main Chamber. Some rooms have red or black decoration in spirals or hexagons; one wall drawing is meant to be a bull.

The whole complex, which covers an area of 800 square meters (8,600 square feet), is estimated to have contained 7,000 bodies. The site is undoubtedly ancient Malta's best-preserved monument.

The **Tarxien** (TAHR-sheen) temples, only 400 meters (1,312 feet) away, date from the same era as the lower levels of the Hal Saflieni Hypogeum, but their garden setting makes a complete contrast. The temples were discovered by a farmer who was having trouble ploughing his fields because of all the megalithic stones in the earth: hearing of the man's find, the archaeologist Sir Themistocles Zammit jumped at the chance to uncover the site, which he excavated between 1915 and 1919.

The temples were built at different times, from about 3200 to 2500 B.C. As you enter you'll see a plan of the area, and some carved stones and stone artefacts. The first temple you come to has replicas of lively bas-relief carvings—spirals, sheep, goats, pigs, cattle, and the lower half of a "fat lady," whose vast thighs are an inspiration to any weight-watcher.

The second temple has six lobes, or oval bays, off the main axis, instead of the more usual four or five. Part of the floor has been removed to give visitors a view of some of the hundreds of heavy stone balls used as rollers for the huge slabs used to construct the temple—they were left in place as supports.

The third temple of the group is the oldest with, a little farther on, parts of the ancient Ġgantija-period temple.

GOZO

The legendary siren Calypso kept Ulysses enthralled here for seven blissful years, and Gozo still enchants people who like its sleepy pace and rustic charm. In the local language, it's known as *Għawdex* (pronounced "Ow-dehsh").

Malta's smaller sister is only 14 km (9 miles) long by 7 km (4 miles) wide, boasts a population of almost 30,000, and its own distinctive character. Gozitans are proud of their island and quite tolerant of Maltese jokes depicting them as country cousins. They can afford to be tolerant: Many Gozitans have made it to the top in business, government and the Church, in Malta and the world beyond.

Gozo is greener than Malta, with neat terraces, dry stone walls, and flat-topped hills. In every direction, the towers and domes of churches are silhouetted against the sky. The islanders are great church-builders: many of the parish churches are big enough for a city of half a million people, and there are dozens of little wayside chapels. A day in Gozo is constantly punctuated by church bells ringing their various messages.

While 20th-century traffic has taken over the few main roads, life still goes on much as it did a century ago. For one thing, big agricultural equipment wouldn't be much use on the narrow terraces. The people of Gozo live mainly on farming, with excellent crops of tomatoes, potatoes, melons, oranges, and figs. The

> **The painted-on eyes of a *luzzu*, a fishing boat, are the eyes of Osiris, an Egyptian god of protection.**

fishing fleet puts to sea whenever the weather permits and, despite declining stocks, still manages to bring in a tasty and varied catch.

Activity centres around the hub and capital, Victoria, although there is much to see elsewhere. Gozo has not only interesting churches, but also great Neolithic temples at Ġgantija and spectacular scenery. Beach life can be beautiful here, but it's also simple—you won't find a sophisticated cabana setting. There are few luxury hotels, but some of the small hotels and restaurants are delightful, and a growing number of farmhouses are being converted into holiday homes.

Gozo does have an airstrip, only a helicopter pad. However, you can reach the island by ferry from Sa Maison, near Valletta, or from Ċirkewwa, or on a private boat or on an excursion from Sliema—whichever route you take, the short crossing is a pleasure. You'll pass the island of Comino with its watchtower; Comino's one hotel stands above a bay on the other side of the island. The name Comino comes from the herb cumin, which once grew in abundance there. The uninhabited islet of Cominotto partly shields Comino's idyllic Blue Lagoon—a magnet for excursion boats in summer.

Mġarr (im-JAHRR), on the southeast coast, where you'll arrive on Gozo, is everything an island harbour should be, alive with bobbing *luzzu* boats and visiting yachts. The tall steeple on the hill above belongs to a 19th-century church, Our Lady of Lourdes. On the headland is Fort Chambray, built in the mid 18th century by a French knight.

The ups and downs of Gozo's history broadly reflect Malta's. First the builders of prehistoric temples at Ġgantija, then the Phoenicians, Romans, Arabs and Normans, Turkish raiders, the Knights of St. John, and finally the British—all have left their mark.

By the side of the road between Mġarr and Victoria, **Gozo Heritage** is a cleverly designed evocation of island history. You are led by sound and lights through a series of rooms, each one a dramatic tableau. (There's an admission charge.) In an adjoining shop you can sometimes watch craftspeople working.

Victoria

The British renamed Gozo's bustling centre during Queen Victoria's jubilee in 1897, but Gozitans still use its old Arab name, Rabat ("city").

Just 6 km (4 1/2 miles) from Mġarr in the centre of the island, the town has a citadel standing high on a bluff, a landmark visible from most parts of the island.

The broad main street is **Republic Street** with the bank and post office. During the Feast of the Assumption on 15 August (and also on the Feast of St. George, on the third Sunday in July) colourful horse and donkey races are run up Republic Street, when everybody turns out to see their friends race in sulkies or ride bareback; the scene can be hilarious. Also on the Feast of the Assumption, nearby Rundle Gardens are the scene of a charming country fair.

It-Tokk, the attractive tree-shaded square with a war monument in the middle, is edged with little shops, tunnel-

Mġarr, Gozo's charming little harbour,
is where ferries and hydrofoils arrive from Malta.

shaped bars, and a bank. On one side is the 18th-century St. James's Church, on the other a rounded building, dating from 1733, that once housed the Banca Giuratale; today it's a tourist information office and a haven for locals wishing to read their newspapers. Any morning the square is full of activity from the open-air market. In the evenings it swarms with people again, walking slowly up and down for the *passeggiata,* the pre-dinner social hour. At market times, you'll see a lavish display of fish, fruit and vegetables, and hear lively banter between shoppers and sellers.

The **old town** behind It-Tokk is charmingly picturesque, with narrow alleys, simple old houses, and women making lace in their doorways. In St. George's Street almost every house has a plaque of the saint slaying the dragon.

Steep steps lead up to the cathedral within the citadel at Victoria on Gozo.

St. George's Church, on its eponymous square, is a fine example of Baroque architecture, elaborately gilded and decorated. The **painting** by Mattia Preti over the choir altar shows St. George with his foot poised in victory on the dragon's head, his white charger by his side. The July festival is quite a bash, and there is a good deal of rivalry between St. George's Church and the cathedral, whose festival is the Assumption, on 15 August.

The **cathedral** stands within the citadel. Behind the austere stone façade, guarded by two bronze cannons, is a surprisingly elaborate interior. Built by Lorenzo Gafà between 1697 and 1711, it has a convincing *trompe l'oeil* dome painted by Antonio Manuele; the real dome was never finished for lack of funds.

On the left as you enter is a modern statue of the Virgin in pale blue and white, her eyes and hands raised heavenward, posed on an ornate and heavy silver pedestal. It is carried all around town during the Festival of the Assumption. The Cathedral Museum houses collections of church ornaments, sacred vestments, and paintings.

To the south of the cathedral stands the Bondi Palace, containing the **Gozo Museum of Archaeology,** built around an inner courtyard. Among the exhibits are Punic jewellery, *amphorae* (jars) from Roman shipwrecks, the 12th-century tombstone of an Arab girl, Majmuna, with a touching inscription, and shards and relics from various eras, especially prehistoric phases. A model of Ġgantija as well as a large phallic symbol from one of Ġgantija's temples, will provide a good introduction to the temples you can see at Xaghra.

Up a little street on the other side of the cathedral you'll come to the **Folklore Museum,** where some traditional implements and costumes are displayed in three restored old houses. Farther up this alley, and also reached by practically every other path in Victoria, there are steps leading to the ramparts of the **citadel.** In the 15-minute walk around the ramparts you will be presented with marvellous **views** all over Gozo, with flat-topped houses edging the meandering roads and a church on nearly every hilltop. The ramparts were strengthened after the brutal Turkish incursion and kidnappings of 1551.

After failing in an assault against the knights in Malta, Dragut, the North African pirate (see page 22), attacked

Gozo, carrying off almost the whole population of 6,000 islanders and selling them into slavery. Gozo was invaded many times by the Turks in the 16th century, and the stone dwellings of the citadel were gradually abandoned. The rubble has been deserted for years, but a full-scale restoration programme is now under way.

☞ Ġgantija Temples

To reach Gozo's most important prehistoric site, take the road to Xagħra (SHAH-rah). Just south of town, inside a fenced enclosure, you'll find the most imposing temple group in the Maltese islands.

Ġgantija was excavated at various times between 1827 and 1953. Like most prehistoric temples in Malta, the two here face southeast: the older and larger is on the left as you approach them. It dates from around 3600 to 3300 B.C. (see page 64 for a comment on dating), during the period sometimes called the Copper Age (precursor to the Bronze Age), although there was no copper on Malta or Gozo then.

Typical of this type of temple, the façade is slightly concave. The entry is flanked by two orthostats (upright stones), a big slab, and a concave stone where worshippers may have washed their feet. The left part of the façade is constructed with immense coralline limestone slabs that rise to a height of about 6 meters (19 1/2 feet).

The inside walls and the decoration are of the softer globigerina limestone. Five lobe-shaped apses contain a number of interesting features, including libation holes, an oracle hole, and stones carved with swirling patterns.

One stone block once supported the huge phallic symbol that now resides in the Gozo Archaeological Museum. The three rear apses were probably restricted to priests and the end apse has impressively high walls, which curve inward to make a semidome. The altar, with holes that were perhaps used for draining animal blood, has blocks with pitted decoration, typical of the period.

The smaller and later temple is less interesting. Here the rear apse and altar are a mere niche. A walk round the whole site shows the skill of early builders. Some of the huge blocks of limestone measure 5.5 meters (18 feet) long and weigh up to 25 tons. You can only marvel at the technical feat performed by a people, who supposedly knew no mathematics, in raising these structures.

Towns and Villages

Xagħra, northwest of Ġgantija, was inhabited in prehistoric times. It's a pleasant town with an exuberantly decorated, Baroque-style 19th-century church. Signs point to Xerri's Cave and Ninu's Cave, which you can visit to view odd-shaped stalactites and stalagmites.

At the northeast corner of the Xagħra plateau, with its superb view over to Ramla Bay on the right, you come to **Calypso's Cave,** where Ulysses supposedly dallied with the fair siren. One wonders what either Calypso or Ulysses saw in this place, apart from the view, as the narrow stairs lead to a singularly unimpressive and murky hole.

Ramla Bay has Gozo's biggest golden-sand beach. It has a simple bar in summer, and plenty of space to sun yourself, despite its popularity. Għajn Barrani, northwest of Ramla, is accessible only by a primitive road that stops at the head of a cliff. After the road ends you have to scramble down: The setting is lovely, however, and the rocks flat and perfect for sunbathing.

Xewkija, just off the main road from Victoria to Mġarr, is a rather plain town with an amazing church begun in 1951 and completed 30 years later. Built to a classical design in golden globigerina limestone, it is a typical Gozitan accomplishment, realized by sheer labour and the devotion of the town's 3,500 citizens. The **dome** rivals the one at Mosta in Malta as one of the largest in the world. The parishioners built their new church right over the old one, removing the first when the new building could be used. Some of its features are preserved in a side-chapel.

Xlendi (SHLEHN-dee) is reached by a small road leading south west from Victoria. It occupies a lovely natural site, well worth the 3 km (2 mile) trip from the island capital, though it can be crowded. On the way, you'll see hilly pastoral scenery and, on the left, a massive washhouse from the knights' time, adorned with the arms of the order. Xlendi stands at the seaward end of a long and beautifully terraced *wied,* or valley.

The pastel houses of the town are tucked away at the head of a narrow bay protected by two tall, rocky promontories. High on the southern side there's a great growth of apartments, but the shore is a favourite spot for swimming. The cliffs opposite are for walkers: follow them along the main path to its end, through a natural rock garden dotted with wildflowers in winter and spring, and you'll come to an old rock-cut boat-house. With hotels, cafés, and restaurants, Xlendi enjoys its status as a favourite excursion haunt, where little shops sell lace, knitwear, and other local products.

An adjacent road out of Victoria leads to **Sannat,** a tiny town well-known for its lace-making. Just beyond it is the Ta' Ċenċ hotel, built from native stone and discreetly hidden among the trees. You'll find it along a short walk from the dramatic **Ta' Ċenċ** cliffs and the huge new reservoir that is a boon to the neighbouring towns. The rough, stony countryside between the hotel and the cliff tops is a good area for finding prehistoric "cart tracks" (see page 14).

There are spectacular clifftop walks near Ta' Ċenċ on Gozo.

All roads lead from Victoria, and Marsalforn is about 4 km (2 1/2 miles) to the northeast of Victoria. On the way you'll see several old windmills and, crowning a peak to the left, a statue of Christ. Once a quiet fishing harbour, **Marsalforn** has become a popular holiday centre because of its opportunities for diving, sailing, and swimming off the short, sandy beaches and inviting rock ledges.

Walk or drive west along the coastal tracks to see strange sculpted salt pans, or head inland through rugged country to village of **Żebbuġ** (ZEHB-booj), which has a traditional church and good views. You can also take the wider road from Victoria to Żebbuġ.

Ask anybody hereabouts for the house of Sebastian Axiak, a local farmer who turned his hand to sculpting and made a big diorama. He died many years ago, but the family is still happy to greet visitors and display his creation, a charming potpourri of Christian lore, village scenes, and belltowers from all over the world.

West of Victoria is Gozo's least populated and, some say, prettiest area. The latest part of the island to have been settled, it was long known as the "desert." Hikers should aim for one of Gozo's less-visited beauty spots—the gorge of **Wied il-Għasri,** which runs down to the sea.

On a side road between Għammar and Għarb is a vast neo-Romanesque church, **Ta' Pinu,** built between 1920 and 1936.

Natural arches and outcroppings add drama to the spectacular coastline near Dwejra.

The main attraction of this incongruous affair is the sites association with miracles. On 22 June 1883, two cousins, Carmela Grima and Francesco Portelli, were visiting a chapel (built in 1534) that once stood on the site when they heard a mysterious voice urging them to say three *aves*. The two prayed for Francesco's desperately ill mother, who miraculously recovered, and from then on the miracles multiplied. Ta' Pinu is still a shrine and place of pilgrimage. A path opposite is lined with marble statues depicting the Stations of the Cross.

Nearby, just outside Għarb, a little museum houses objects made by the pious, Carmela and Francesco. To see these curiosities, seek out the priest at Ta' Pinu, who can arrange to open the museum.

Għarb (Arabic for "west") is the picture-perfect and peaceful Gozitan village, with a lovely Baroque church on its main square, pastel house fronts, a tiny village shop, and little else to do but watch the women making lace. The square is decorated with colored pillars and lights at *festa* time in early July.

Strong Medicine

The plant growing on Fungus Rock that the knights so valued is not actually a fungus at all, but a parasitic species called Cynomorium coccineum. Drawing nourishment from the roots of other plants, it pushes up orange-red, leafless spikes. The knights discovered it had haemostatic properties (controlling the flow of blood) and was useful in treating intestinal disorders, a skill for which Malta was renowned almost until modern times. The stuff was thought so precious that anyone found even attempting to raid the rock could be sentenced to death or—a fate scarcely less dire—the galleys.

Take the small road just south of Għarb through San Lawrenz down to **Dwejra** to see a big outcrop in the water— so big, in fact, it almost entirely blocks the entrance to Qawra Bay. Named General's Rock, it's more often called Fungus Rock after a plant found there and prized by the knights for its curative powers.

The bay below is dominated by Qawra Tower, built in 1651. The road ends near a chapel and an extraordinary rock promontory, where you can walk across a natural arch over the sea. Down a track to the right is the **Inland Sea,** a grandiose name for a salt water lagoon linked by a natural tunnel to the sea. When the sea is calm, you should be able to swim through without too much effort in about 10 minutes. Some boat-houses along the beach are open in summer as snack-bars or little shops.

Fast-growing **Nadur,** 5 km (3 miles) east of Victoria, is the second largest town in Gozo, and the richest. The people are proud of their church, built by G. Bonnici in the 18th century, restored in the 19th, and elaborately decorated. The town is situated at quite an altitude for Gozo—more than 150 meters (492 feet) above sea level (the name Nadur means "summit" in Arabic).

For isolated rock bathing in a pretty setting, you can take a narrow road north of Nadur (locals will gladly point the way to passing motorists), then park at the end of the road and walk down past orange groves sheltered by bamboo fences to the pretty coves in the area know as **San Blas.** Another branch of the same road from Nadur takes you to the charming, small fishing harbour of **Daħlet Qorrot,** where boat-houses are carved out of the cliffs. **Qala** (khAH-lah) is a country town, and its windmill is the last one working in Gozo. Farther on are quarries that supplied the stone for the Roman Catholic Cathedral of Liverpool.

WHAT TO DO

SPORTS

The choice is yours. Malta's climate makes the islands a paradise for sports and activities. Aware of the latest trend towards healthy exercise, many of the bigger hotels have added tennis and squash courts, gyms, saunas, and indoor pools to their range of facilities. Naturally, water sports come first in summer, and the cooler months are perfect for walking the coastal paths and hills.

Swimming

Swimming is free everywhere on Malta except at a few clubs where you can have the benefits of a terrace restaurant, changing rooms and showers. In popular spots you can rent a beach chair or mat and beach umbrella.

There are about a dozen small sandy beaches on Malta, most notably at Golden Bay, Ġnejna Bay, Paradise Bay, and Mellieħa Bay. But even prettier scenery and better snorkelling can be enjoyed at the rocky beach sites, such as Peter's Pool, Marsaskala, Għar Lapsi, around St. Paul's Bay, and the seaward side of Sliema, though the beach here can be crowded.

On Gozo, the only sizeable stretch of sand is Ramla Bay, and there are tiny beaches—or plenty of rocks from which to swim from—at San Blas, Daħlet Qorrot, Hondoq, Mġarr ix-Xini, Xlendi, the "Inland Sea," and Marsalforn.

Waterskiing and Paragliding

You can get a tow and take off at all the main beaches and bigger resort hotels. If you plan to do much water-skiing, try to negotiate a "package deal" price—paying for lots of single trips is expensive.

Windsurfing

As popular on Malta as it is on any holiday coast, windsurfing is well-organized, with boards for hire at hotels and beaches, and beginners' lessons are available. For experts, international competitions include the Malta to Sicily race in April. The sheltered bays—Mellieħa, St. Paul's, Marsamxett, Marsaskala, St. Thomas, St. George's, and Ramla—often ripple with coloured sails.

Scuba Diving and Snorkelling

The snorkelling possibilities are good everywhere you can swim, and especially off rocky shores, where the water can be wonderfully clear. If you don't bring your own masks, snorkels and flippers, you can buy or rent them at beach centres.

The Maltese islands can claim some of the world's best diving and, except for a few winter storms, it's a year-round sport. You must have a permit from the Department of Health, Merchants Street, Valletta (you'll need a medical certificate, two photos, and a logbook to get one). To dive independently from a diving school you must be able to show advanced qualifications.

You'll find licensed schools at St. Julian's, St. Paul's Bay/ Qawra, Marsaskala, Paradise Bay, Valletta and Gzira, on Comino, and at Marsalforn, Xlendi, and Xewkija on Gozo. They can give instruction to all levels, and take care of the administrative details as well.

An excellent leaflet, *Malta—Mecca for Divers*, is published by the National Tourist Office, giving addresses, regulations, a guide to prices, and a description of main sites.

Boating and Sailing

Malta has a long season of fine sailing weather, and if you don't come in your own boat you can rent anything from a luxury craft to a dinghy. Marsamxett Harbour is the main centre, and there are marinas at Ta 'Xbiex and Msida and full repair facilities on Manoel Island, where you can find out about berthing and charter. The Royal Malta Yacht Club on Manoel Island accepts temporary members. Regattas are held from April to November.

Even if you don't sail yourself, be sure to take the opportunity to get afloat. There are countless cruises and excursions to every part of the coast, some in glass-bottomed boats from which you can view the underwater scene.

Fishing

Fishing is free to all and a licence is not required, but a little politeness goes a long way, so ask the locals whether they mind before you fish from their favourite rock. If you want to go out on a boat, inquire at one of the harbours, especially Marsaxlokk or St. Paul's Bay (and Mġarr or Marsalforn on Gozo). Spearfishing without a licence is forbidden.

Walking

Almost every distant point on the islands is reached by some sort of track, though you may not be happy about one of the reasons—to give access to bird-trappers and hunters. The sign "RTO" is short for *reservato,* meaning "private hunting ground." Wear strong shoes or thick-soled trainers, so you'll be comfortable along the rougher tracks and where scrambling over sharp-edged eroded limestone.

Some of the most scenic routes on Malta are the ridges and cliff-top paths of the north and west coasts. All of Gozo's coast and hills are well worth exploring. The northwestern end of the island has many beautiful areas that can be reached only on foot.

The Marsa Sports Club

Situated between Valletta's Grand Harbour and the airport, this centre has tennis, squash, billiards, a pool, an 18-hole golf course, as well as a bar club-house and restaurant. Visitors can join on a weekly basis, or for longer. Horse racing (mostly trotting but also a few flat races) takes place at Marsa racecourse each Sunday from October to May, and stables in the area offer riding facilities.

Malta provides ample opportunity to get afloat.

Other Sports

There are indoor bowling centres at Msida and St. Julian's west of Valletta's, and you might see the traditional Maltese bowls (*bocci*) in the villages. You can go rollerskating at St. Julian's, and indulge in archery, table tennis and badminton at the Marsa Club. The strong-swimming locals can be found playing water polo wherever there's a suitable pool.

Playing, watching, reading, and talking about football is a national pastime. Except in high summer, dozens of teams compete in league and cup competitions. International and other important matches take place at the National Stadium at Ta' Qali near Mdina.

SHOPPING

There are few big stores on Malta, and you'll probably do most of your buying in small shops and markets. Prices are generally rea-

Malta's doorways are ideally suited to making and displaying lace.

sonable, and the one quoted is the real price— haggling is not a way of life here, though it can be worth negotiating terms at outdoor bric-a-brac stalls or at small jeweller's shops.

Best Buys

Silver, especially delicate filigree work, is extremely attractive and enticingly priced. The only problem is choosing from the wonderful displays of Maltese crosses, earrings, necklaces, little boats, and boxes. The same shapes are also fashioned in gold.

Lace, made in Malta and especially on Gozo by women who often sit working in their doorways, is an ideal gift or souvenir—light and unbreakable. Creating the borders for handkerchieves, placemats, and tablecloths, it can be fine and intricate. But look carefully before buying, and compare examples: some of the work can be rather rough.

You can see almost every kind of craft practised on the islands at the Crafts Village, Ta' Qali, near Mdina, housed in the buildings of a former airfield. The **glass** makers here mould and blow remarkable shapes in subtle blends of colours— turquoise blue, bottle green, and varying shades of brown. This particular style was started by two Englishmen and enthusiastically adopted by local artisans to make ornaments and vases, glasses, decanters, and ashtrays. Other glass works can be visited on Manoel Island and near Għarb on Gozo.

Look through the range of **pottery** and **ceramics**—you'll probably find something that appeals to you. Another workshop at Ta' Qali cuts and polishes "Malta Stone," a banded brown-and-white calcite, into bookends, ashtrays, and souvenirs.

Hand- and machine-knitted **woollens** are on sale in shops and stalls all over the islands. The weather may not be appropriate, but you might find an Aran-style sweater, a pullover, or a shawl at a fair price. Feel the wool: it can vary from soft and angoralike to quite hard and prickly.

The crafts centre just across the square from St. John's Co-Cathedral concentrates the islands' products in a single display, ranging from original folk art to garish kitsch. The best spots to shop on Gozo are at the Citadel Crafts Centre and in the crafts village at Ta' Dbiegi near San Lawrenz.

Other good buys include locally made cotton swimwear and underwear, jeans, printed and plain T-shirts, and various interesting hand towels.

FESTIVALS

The Maltese will celebrate at the drop of a hat, and fortunately there are plenty of opportunities to do so. In fact, it is a duty for each parish to mark its saint's day with a joyous *festa*, and since there are 64 parishes in Malta and 14 in Gozo, the calendar is full.

A 'xalata takes place on the Monday after a festa. It is a light picnic at the beach to relax from all the activities.

It just so happens that most *festi* fall during the summer months. The main celebrations are usually moved to the weekend following the actual saint's day, but they are preceded by three days of prayer services. Thanksgiving masses are held in the morning, in churches decorated with flowers, huge silver candlesticks, and red silk damask hangings. Brass bands parade through town and men carry a statue of the saint in procession through the packed crowds. There's a concert in the main square, and an often excellent fireworks display (generally timed for the Saturday night). Exact dates for the whole year's *festi* can be obtained from the National Tourist Office.

Apart from local festivals, there are a dozen or so fixed national public holidays and one, Good Friday, which is moveable. **Carnival,** the spell of merrymaking before Lent, therefore also moves from year to year, but generally falls in late February. Grotesque masks, decorated floats, parties, and traditional dances (including the *parata* that commemorates the knights' victory over the Turks in 1565) add up to a five-day feast.

Good Friday is marked by processions of hooded penitential figures carrying statues of scenes from the Passion, and men and women dressed up as various biblical characters. **Easter Sunday** sees more processions celebrating the risen Christ, and children take their *figolla* (iced marzipan cakes) to be blessed.

The **Commemoration of 7 June 1919** is a national holiday, and later that month is the **Imnarja** folklore festival, held on the Feast of St. Peter and St. Paul (29 June) in Valletta's Buskett Gardens.

On 8 September, the feast day for Our Lady of Victories, the celebrations of victory in the two Great Sieges include a **Regatta** in Grand Harbour. Muscular oarsmen battle for prizes and honour amid a bedlam of sirens, horns, and cheers (the sailors' turn comes in the **Autumn Races** organized by the Royal Malta Yacht Club in October). Later in September **Independence Day** is celebrated on 21 September.

Republic Day on 13 December is marked by a public holiday and parades, music and fireworks, particularly in Vittoriosa. The year's celebrations climax with Christmas—an occasion for family gatherings—and New Year's Eve parties.

ENTERTAINMENT

Nightlife is mainly limited to the resort areas—Sliema, St. Julian's, and Buġibba/Qawra—where there's plenty of activity. The scene is mostly quite informal, centred on the handful of discos and the bars and pubs that put on entertainment.

Theatre and Concerts

Valletta's beautiful Manoel Theatre stages plays in English and Maltese, concerts by the local orchestra, and some ballet or opera during a season that lasts from October to May. Visiting international soloists and groups appear there, too—they say

*Disco to a Maltese beat—the lighting effects are modern,
but the folk costumes are ages old.*

how much they like its intimate atmosphere and acoustics. In the summer there may be outdoor performances of plays in San Anton Gardens. You can stay informed about schedules by reading *What's On*. Occasional plays and other shows are put on in Gozo's two theatres as well, during the winter months.

Cinema

For the latest releases try the "Eden Century" in St. George's Bay (St. Julian's). Sliema and Valletta have a few cinemas, with the occasional one to be found in other towns. Gozo's cinemas are in Victoria. Films are mostly in English, with a few in Italian, and programmes change frequently.

Nightlife

You can go to dinner dances in many of the big hotels, or a buffet and cabaret combination in St. Julian's. Some of the pubs in Paceville put on entertainment, and many bars (both in hotels and out) have live music you can dance to. Malta by Night tours, barbecue-and-folklore evenings, medieval banquets, and the like have been cooked up as excursions to provide further variety for holidaymakers.

Discos are a magnet to the young. Some are high-tech with intricate light shows; others are just an open space beneath the stars on summer nights, when all discos are at their liveliest. Although most nightclubs close at midnight or thereabouts, several in Paceville keep going until the early hours of the morning. Some charge an entrance fee.

The palatial Casino, at Dragonara Point, St. George's Bay (St. Julian's) features roulette, blackjack, and slot machines, plus a bar and restaurant. It opens at 8:00 P.M. and closes in the small hours, depending on the action. Take your passport if you want to join the dedicated or casual gamblers, or even just to look.

EATING OUT

A glance at the market stalls you will see throughout Malta will tell you of the possibilities of the foods that can be enjoyed on the islands. The best of Maltese food is full of Mediterranean colour, freshness, and flavour—juicy tomatoes, bright green and red peppers, squash, salad crops all the year round, and the freshest of fish. These ingredients are used in a genuine Maltese cooking that does exist, though you have to look for it among all the influences from Italy (pasta muscles in everywhere) and Britain (fish and chips and an unfortunate touch of blandness).

> The slow simmering of food dates back to the times where gas and electricity was not available. Because of limited amounts of firewood food was placed in pots over a *kenur*, a little stone hearth and cooked slowly.

It is possible to eat well for a reasonable price, especially simple dishes like fresh *fettuccine* in a sauce, or grilled swordfish. Maltese bread, with a crisp brown crust and soft "holey" inside, is a treat, but white French-style bread and sliced loaves tend to be somewhat tasteless.

The choice of restaurants on Malta is vast, and Gozo has a good selection, too. You'll find everything from the most basic, with plastic tables and strip lighting (where it's possible to eat a local pie for next to nothing), right up to an elegant terrace setting overlooking the sea with polished service and superb cuisine. You'll also find Chinese, Japanese, Greek, or Turkish food, as authentic as the chefs—from China, Japan, Greece and Turkey—can make it.

Restaurants are classified into four grades by the government. This system generally corresponds to price ranges, though the ratings may not be a reliable guide to quality.

Hours of service are quite conventional: lunch is usually served between noon and 2:00 P.M. and 2:30 P.M. and dinner between 7:00 P.M. and 10:00 P.M.

Breakfast in hotels may be continental, "English" (with a cooked dish), or buffet-style. The price of breakfast is normally included in the room rate, except, paradoxically, in the most expensive places.

Starters

You'll often see appetizers and hors d'oeuvres listed, as the Italians do, as *antipasti*. They may include slices of local pepper sausage, raw or cooked mixed vegetables, Parma ham (or a similar style), and melon or prawn cocktail. Soups include *kawlata* or *minestra*, which are hearty concoctions of everything in the kitchen garden and more filling than the Italian *minestrone*. *Consommés*, fresh (and tinned) tomato soup, and mulligatawny (from India via Britain) are featured on many

The best, freshest, and most authentic fare in Malta usually comes from the sea.

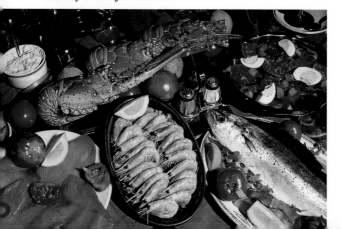

menus. If you like something spicy, look out for fish soups; the best come laden with chunks of different fish and shellfish and laced with garlic and chili peppers.

Pasta

There are many Italian restaurants offering a variety of pasta dishes, some of them excellent, and the numerous international restaurants also usually have a pasta section on the menu. You'll see all varieties, from the ubiquitous *spaghetti bolognese* to *vermicelli alle vongole* (with clams). In addition to these, there are some genuine Maltese pasta dishes. *Timpana*, when homemade, is a flaky pastry pie filled with macaroni, minced meat, onion, tomato, aubergine, eggs, and cheese. The version sold in snack bars cuts down on everything but the pastry and macaroni—it's economical and filling. *Ravjul* is a local version of *ravioli*.

Fish and Shellfish

Landed that very morning and as fresh as can be, fish is prime fare in Malta. It is usually served grilled, steamed, fried whole, or *alla Maltese* (with a tomato and green pepper sauce).

Lampuka is Malta's "own" fish, which gathers under offshore floats put out specially for it. The opening of the season (it begins in late August and lasts until November) is a big moment, when the fishermen raise their little triangular flags in salute. A kind of dolphinfish (nothing to do with dolphins!), *lampuka* is served grilled, in a casserole with wine and herbs, in a pie (*torta tal-lampuki*), or fried, then cooked in a pastry shell along with onion, tomatoes, cauliflower, spinach, and perhaps olive oil and walnuts.

Octopus and squid (*calamari*) and cuttlefish are often served up as salads, spicy stews, or stuffed. Grilled swordfish (*pix-xispada*) and tuna steaks are good standbys. Other fine fish may hide behind unfamiliar names: *dott* (stone bass) and *ċerna* (grouper) can be excellent. Various types of prawns are popular, and lobster, as in most places, is expensive.

Meat

Carnivores can find a T-bone or a pepper steak on most menus, but it is worth looking for something more typically Maltese such as *braġoli*, a slice of beef rolled round a filling of bacon, breadcrumbs, egg, parsley, and a touch of garlic, fried, then simmered in onions and wine.

The islanders will often serve casseroles of beef and lamb with potatoes and onions in their homes, and that's what "roast beef Maltese-style" means on menus. However, most local meat dishes—braised pork, ox tongue in wine sauce, and fricassé of meatballs and sweetbreads—rarely appear on the menu at all. The only meat dish most people, locals included, used to think of as typically Maltese was *fenek* (rabbit), which was either fried or stewed with wine and garlic. That's now changing, with the growth of interest in national cuisine and the opening of several restaurants offering it.

You'll find good veal *(vitello)* on Italian-style menus, and the chicken is reliable. It's probably the British liking for roast lamb and lamb chop—not a Maltese flare for preparing them—that make them a continuing staple on island menus.

Salads and Vegetables

Good fresh produce is always available. No matter how bad the drought, ingenious irrigation systems trickle water to the terraces and greenhouses. You should find good spinach, cour-

A red pillar-box and Queen Victoria may remind you of Britain. The pleasure of sitting in an open-air café probably won't.

gettes (zucchini), and tomatoes. Baby new potatoes in butter are delicious and so are the chips (French fries) and baked potatoes. Other well-known Maltese staples include stuffed green peppers and succulent aubergines (eggplants), fried or baked.

Cheeses

Here you're close enough to the source to get a variety of excellent Italian cheeses. Also look out for the different kinds of sheep's-milk cheeses (*ġbejna*) made in Malta and Gozo. Mostly small and round, these cheeses can be dry and hard, but they are also available in brine and capers, or rolled in black peppercorns. Gozo specializes in goat's-milk cheese (*ġbej-niet*), which can come in the form of roundels.

Desserts and Fruit

There's plenty of Italian-style ice-cream in many flavours, and cake shops and restaurants provide *semifreddo* ice-cream cake confections. Various types of *gâteaux* and *torte* (cakes and tarts) are on many menus. Soft *ricotta* cheese is sometimes used in sweet cheesecakes with fruit or combined with chocolate, cherries, sugar, and almonds to fill little cornets called *kannoli tarrikotta*. *Helwa tat-tork* is ultra sweet, made from sesame flour.

Festivals bring their own special sweet things. At Easter you'll see *figolli* in the shops, iced almond-lemon biscuits cut in various shapes. *Prinjolata* is a combination of sponge fingers, butter cream, and almonds or pinenuts, and decorated with chocolate and cherries.

Fresh fruit makes an ideal dessert: peaches, plums, apricots, and figs in summer, then melons, followed by oranges and tangerines in winter. The strawberry season lasts longer and longer, with new varieties and techniques developed for the export business. And if you haven't yet tried prickly pears now's your chance, but beware of the tiny spines that cover them. Get them on your hands, or worse, in your mouth, and you'll itch for hours. Experts say they don't stick into you when they're wet with the morning dew!

Snacks

It's part of the local way of life to pick up a sandwich, pie, or meat-filled pastry at a tiny snack bar or a stall in the street. *Pastizzi* or *qassata,* various flaky pastry turnovers or pies with a filling of *ricotta*, peas and onion, or anchovies are especially popular. In local bars you'll see customers enjoying a plate of snails with their beer.

Drinks and Wines

> Hubz bizzejt is a bread rubbed with tomatoes until it turns red, then topped with olive oil, herbs and capers.

The fruit juices are excellent, especially the fresh ones, of course. Try the pear, peach, apricot, and exotic mixtures. The usual soft drinks are available: a local brand called *Kinnie* is rather like an orange-flavoured cola. Maltese beer and lager are good and inexpensive; imports tend to cost about twice as much.

Imported fine or ordinary wines can be found both in stores and on restaurant lists, but Malta itself produces some very drinkable wines sold for a much lower price. The reds are quite full-bodied, although the cheaper kind can be rather acidic. Four famous brands are *Marsovin Special Reserve, Lachryma Vitis, Farmers,* and *Festa*. Look for *La Valette* and four- or five-year-old *Marsovin Cabernet Sauvignon.*

The same four brand names appear on white wines. They are mostly dry and fruity, and refreshing when well chilled. The more respectable of Gozo's wines include Velson's red and white. The Ġgantija wines, both red and white, are sweeter. Watch out for the high alcohol content of some of the local wines. Also beware of the mild to drastic laxative effect that drinking too much of them can have.

Help with the Menu

The list below contains a selection of the words (Maltese, Italian, and French) that you might come across on a Maltese menu.

abbachio, agnello, agneau	lamb
aglio, ail	garlic
anitra, canard	duck
boeuf, manzo	beef
braġoli, bragioli	beef olive
carciofi, qaqoċċ	artichoke
ċerna	grouper fish (*mérou*)
coniglio, lapin, fenek	rabbit
dolce	dessert
espadon, pesce spada	swordfish
fagioli, fagiolini, haricots	beans
formaggio, fromage	cheese
funghi, champignons	mushrooms
ġbejna	Maltese sheep's milk
homard, astice	lobster
lampuka	dolphinfish special to Malta
melanzana	aubergine, eggplant
naranja	orange
patate, pommes de terre	potatoes
pesce, poisson	fish
piselli, perits pois	peas
prosciutto, jambon	ham
salsa	sauce
pâtes	pasta
tonn, tonno, thon	tuna (tunny)
uove, oeufs	eggs
vongole	clams

INDEX

Numbers in bold refer to the main entry listed.

Where there is more than
   one set of references, the
   one in bold refers to the
   main entry. Page numbers
   in italic refer to an
   illustration.

HANDY TRAVEL TIPS

An A–Z Summary of Practical Information

A

ACCOMMODATION (See also YOUTH HOSTELS, and RECOMMENDED HOTELS beginning on page 130)

Malta offers everything from luxury hotels to simple guest houses. They are rated according to comfort and amenities by the Hotels and Catering Establishments Board, which also puts out various brochures listing all details. Hotel categories range from five-star (the most luxurious) to one-star (the simplest); holiday complexes and aparthotels are rated first, second, or third class; guest houses as first or second class. Don't take these ratings as an exact guide to quality. You may find that a warm welcome at a so-called second-class guest house may outweigh the 24-hour room service at a five-star hotel.

Self-catering possibilities. You may prefer to rent an apartment, villa, or converted farmhouse for your holiday. Prices and amenities vary, but your travel agent will have brochures detailing choices and prices. The National Tourism Organization can also provide lists. It's unwise to rent from someone you encounter casually: there are some unscrupulous owners who overcharge and don't provide what they promise.

People have favourite accommodations to which they return to year after year, and travel agencies may take all the rooms in the hotel of your choice before you've booked. So reserve early to be sure of getting the accommodation you want.

AIRPORT

The Maltese islands are served by Luqa Airport, some 6 km (3 1/2 miles) south of Valletta, a driving time of about 15 minutes. The airport can take jumbo jets, and is used by Air Malta and some of the other international airlines. Customs formalities are fairly simple, with the usual red and green channels. The currency-exchange counter is open 24 hours a day. The airport has an air-conditioned restaurant, a snack bar, bookstall, and car hire desks. The duty-free shops sell jewellery, tobacco, perfume, wines, and spirits—and you can also buy these items on arrival in Malta as well as at the time of departure. An information counter helps with inquiries and problems. The airport post office is open Monday through Saturday, 7:00 A.M. to 7:00 P.M.

The bus stop for Valletta is a two-minute walk from the terminal building. Some hotels run an airport minibus service, and taxis are available.

There's no airport on Gozo, though there is a helicopter link (see PUBLIC TRANSPORT–FERRIES for how to get to Gozo).

Note: Summer travellers are advised to reach the airport in good time for their return flight. It is not unknown for flights to be overbooked.

Flight inquiries: tel.	662211/5
	223596
	234149
Reservations	677554
Gozo Heliport	561301
	557905

B

BICYCLE and MOTORCYCLE HIRE

Cycling can be tiring under the summer sun, but the islands' reasonably flat terrain and short distances are well suited to the activity. Cycles can be rented for relatively little, and you can avoid traffic jams and parking problems. For further details, consult the Tourist Organization (see TOURIST INFORMATION OFFICES).

C

CAMPING

There are no organized campsites on Malta or Gozo, and it is illegal to camp on beaches overnight.

CAR HIRE (See also DRIVING)

Major international car-hire firms operate in Malta, and some have desks at the airport. There are also dozens of small companies, some reliable, others less so. Terms are reasonable, and most visitors prefer hiring cars to bringing their own. However, in peak holiday periods early booking is advisable. The smaller firms may offer inadequate cars: insist on a recent model and check the tires and general condition. Full insurance cover is recommended. It is not the universal custom to deliver the car with a full tank of petrol: you may need to buy some as soon as you get it.

To hire a car you need a valid driving licence, and some companies may ask to see your passport. Most agencies set a minimum age of 25 for car hire. Reputable firms accept major credit cards as payment, though some may ask for a cash deposit. The rate on page 123 includes tax and third-party insurance. Full cover will cost extra.

And, before you set off, don't forget to DRIVE ON THE LEFT.

Chauffeur-driven cars. This way of sightseeing is more comfortable than driving yourself on the rather difficult roads—if you can afford it. The charge per hour is high. Some garages impose a minimum rental period of eight hours. Taxis can also be hired by the hour, half-day, or day, with prices ranging wildly, depending on your bargaining skills.

CHILDREN'S MALTA

There aren't very many special attractions for children, but they'll be happy all the same, especially on the beaches. The easy, sandy ones are fine for all ages, though you should keep an eye on very young children and toddlers, as there is not much in the way of lifeguard services. Older children can swim, snorkel, or sail from rocky shores.

For a change, the young can enjoy screaming down the water slides at the Splash Park, Bahar ic-Caghaq, or visiting Popeye Village.

The *festi*, religious festivals, are even more fun for children than for adults. They happen at weekends all summer long (tourist information offices can give you a list of where and when). There are parades, perhaps little fairs, and on Saturday evenings the fireworks can be spectacular. Good displays to watch include the St. George festival in Qormi (khOR-mee) and the St. Nicholas festival in Siggiewi (SEEJ-jee-eh-wee), both in late June, and the mid-August festival in Victoria, Gozo.

Children might like the *Imnarja*, or folklore festival, in Buskett Gardens. Also in late June, just after the folklore festival, there's a donkey race at nearby Rabat. More donkey and horse races are held in July, for the feast of St. George in Victoria, Gozo, and in August, around the feast of the Assumption, on both islands. Carnival parades take place in February. The regatta—boat races to celebrate Our Lady of Victories—is held on 8 September in Valletta's Grand Harbour.

In St. Anton Gardens, Malta, the mini-zoo has a small collection of a few animals and birds.

Baby-sitting services are listed in the local papers and in the *What's On* guide.

CLIMATE

Malta has a typical Mediterranean climate with hot, dry summers and mild, humid winters. Even in winter you can expect a few hours of sunshine most days. The sea is quite warm by May and stays pleasant for swimming until October or even November. In May and from about mid-September to mid-October, the *sirocco* blows in from North Africa, raising the humidity. Sea breezes moderate the heat of summer.

Trees and plants flower early on the island: you'll see "spring" blossoms from December to March. After that, temperatures climb quickly, and the landscape takes on its characteristic parched appearance. Summer is the main tourist season, but increasing numbers of people are taking advantage of lower winter prices to enjoy a break from cold northern Europe.

		J	F	M	A	M	J	J	A	S	O	N	D
Air temperature													
Average daily	°F	59	60	62	66	71	82	83	84	82	67	69	63
maximum*	°C	15	15	16	19	23	27	30	31	28	24	20	17
Average daily	°F	49	49	51	54	59	65	70	71	69	63	57	53
minimum*	°C	19	19	10	12	15	19	21	22	20	17	14	11
Water temperature													
°F			58	58	58	62	65	70	75	76	77	72	67	62
°C			14	14	14	16	18	21	24	26	25	22	19	16

* Maximum temperatures are measured in the early afternoon, minimum temperatures just before sunrise.

CLOTHING

Light and loose cotton clothing is the best daytime wear in the hot summer months. Wear a hat or scarf for protection from the sun, and comfortable shoes or sandals for sightseeing.

The heat, however, doesn't mean you can go around half-dressed. The Maltese disapprove of unseemly dress in public places and beachwear away from the beach. Brief shorts, miniskirts, low-cut or shoulder-baring dresses are prohibited for visiting churches. Women may be handed a scarf to cover their shoulders.

Although bikinis are a common sight on beaches, it is illegal to appear topless or nude, and you risk a fine or worse if you try.

In the evening certain luxury hotels and the Casino require men to wear a jacket and tie, and women may need something dressy. Take a jersey or a wrap for cooler evenings. In winter, pack a light jacket, sweater, raincoat, and umbrella.

COMPLAINTS

If things go wrong, try complaining first to the owner or manager of the establishment. The friendly Maltese invariably try to set things right when you explain your problem. If you are still not satisfied, you can then go to the National Tourist Organization (see TOURIST INFORMATION OFFICES), or call the Organization's special number, 245615, where visitors can lodge complaints. This number is staffed during office hours, but at all other times a recording machine registers calls.

Complaints made to the police will usually be referred back to the Tourist Organization. Complaints about service in hotels or restaurants should be lodged with the Hotels and Catering Establishments Board, tel. 242919.

CRIME

Malta is still relatively crime-free compared with the rest of the world. Tourists are safe almost anywhere, but, sadly, theft is on the increase. It is wise to take the usual precautions. Put your valuables in the hotel safe or, if you've rented a flat, don't leave them in a conspicuous place. Lock your car as a matter of course. Any loss or theft should be reported immediately to the nearest police station, and, if it happened at a hotel, to the hotel management.

The possession, use, and distribution of drugs are all considered criminal offences, punishable by fines or a prison sentence or both.

CUSTOMS and ENTRY FORMALITIES

For stays of up to three months, a valid passport is sufficient for most visitors.

Here's what you can take into Malta duty free and, when returning home, into your own country:

Into:	Cigarettes		Cigars		Tobacco	Spirits		Wine
Malta	200 or 250g of other tobacco products*					1 l	or	1 l
Australia	200	or	250 g	or	250 g	1 l	and	1 l
Canada	200	or	50	or	900 g	1.14	or	1.14
Eire	200	and	50	or	250 g	1 l	and	2 l
N. Zealand	200	or	50	or	250 g	1.14	and	4.5 l
S. Africa	400	and	50	and	250 g	1 l	and	2 l
UK	200	or	50	or	250 g	1 l	and	2 l
USA	200	and	100	and	**	1 l	or	1 l

* of which not more than 50 g in loose tobacco

** a reasonable quantity

Currency restrictions. There's no limit on how much foreign currency a non-resident may bring into Malta (large amounts must be declared upon arrival), but you are entitled to import only Lm 50 in local currency. Visitors may export a maximum of Lm 25 in local currency, plus any remaining foreign currency of the sum they brought in and declared to customs upon arrival.

DISABILITIES

Although there are no state laws requiring new buildings to provide access and special toilet facilities for the disabled, the government has embarked on a large project to modify pavements to create easy access for disabled visitors, in its policy to confirm with EU norms.

About 35% of hotels are equipped to cater for disabled customers. Public transport is not yet equipped but special parking areas exist for private cars.

DRIVING

If you're going to the trouble of taking your car to Malta, you'll need:
• your national driving licence
• car registration papers
• insurance coverage (the most common formula for coverage is the Green Card, an extension to your regular insurance that makes it valid abroad).

Drivers and passengers are required to wear seatbelts. It is wise to carry a red warning triangle in case of an emergency.

Driving conditions. The rules in general follow the United Kingdom: drive on the left, overtake on the right; at roundabouts give way to cars coming from the right.

Speed limits are theoretically 40 km/h (25 mph) in built-up areas, 64 km/h (40 mph) on the larger open roads.

The best policy for visitors is to drive defensively, giving a wide berth to lorries, buses, and aggressive-looking vehicles. Driving in Malta, and especially on Gozo, can be a trial for a newcomer used to order.

In the centre of Valletta some streets are closed to cars, others are one-way, and the rest are usually clogged. It is best to park outside the city and visit it on foot.

Road conditions. Both Malta's and Gozo's main routes, though not always in good repair, are usually wide enough to accommodate two or three vehicles abreast. The roads often have potholes, sometimes repaired by hot tar and a mixture of stones plus a fine dust topping.

Parking. Fines for illegal parking are enforced. Be absolutely sure not to block another car or an exit. There are no parking meters. If you put your car in a car park, give the attendant a small tip.

Traffic police. You don't often see them, but they do patrol in cars or on motorcycles and occasionally stop vehicles for safety or identity checks (especially at night).

Malta

Fuel and oil. Fuel is available in super (98 octane), unleaded, and diesel. Service stations are open from 6:30 A.M. to 6:00 P.M. They are closed on Sundays and holidays, so be sure to fill up the day before.

Breakdowns. Towing and on-the-spot repairs are made by local garages, and spare parts can usually be found for most common makes of car. Malta's mechanics are skilled, as evidenced by all the 40-year-old cars and buses still going strong. If you're renting your car, first call the hire firm, which should send help within the hour.

Accidents. In case of an accident, call the police immediately (dial 191). Do not move your vehicle until the police arrive, since claims are not usually settled unless the police make a report on the spot.

E

ELECTRIC CURRENT

Electric supply is 240 volts 50 cycle AC. Three-pronged British-type plugs and sockets are used. Australian and New Zealand visitors will need an adaptor, and Americans will need an adaptor and a transformer.

EMBASSIES and HIGH COMMISSIONS

Australia:	High Commission, Ta' Xbiex Terrace, Ta' Xbiex; tel. 338201.
Canada:	Embassy (Italy), Via G. Battista De Rossi 27, 00161 Rome; tel. (06) 445981.
New Zealand:	Embassy (Italy), Via Zara, 28, 00198 Rome; tel. (06) 4402928.
UK:	High Commission, 7 St. Anne Street, Floriana; tel. 233134/8.
USA:	Embassy, Development House, St. Anne Street, Floriana; tel. 235960/5.

EMERGENCIES

In case of accident or other emergencies, phone:

Police **191**   Ambulance **196**   Fire **199**

For traffic accidents, see DRIVING.

G

GETTING TO MALTA

Considering the wide variety of fares and the choice of ways in which you can travel to Malta, you are well-advised to consult a reliable travel agent. That way you have the best chance of meeting your timetable and budget.

By Air. There are direct flights to Malta's Luqa Airport (see also page 105) from many European cities and several cities in North Africa. Travellers from elsewhere will normally have to fly to a European capital for connecting flights to Malta. Flying time from the UK is about three hours 15 minutes.

Ask about lower fares for children, youths, students and senior citizens, excursions and night flights, as well as inclusive holidays.

By Rail or Road. If you have the time and plan your journey carefully, the trip by **train**, with ferry connections, can be enjoyable. Travellers from northern Europe will have to change trains at least once in order to reach ferry ports to Malta, either in Milan or Rome. Be sure to make advance reservations if you want a sleeping car or couchette.

Discounted train fares are available to senior citizens, youths, children, and groups. Travel agencies can give you details.

If you are taking your **car** south to Malta, you can travel right across Europe by motorway but you'll have to pay a toll on motorway routes in France, Switzerland, and Italy, and if you use one of the tunnels through the Alps. Putting your car on a train is expensive, but saves on wear and tear, fuel, and tolls.

Ferries. to Malta run from Naples, Reggio di Calabria, and Catania and Syracuse in Sicily. All carry both cars and passengers. In addition, a fast catamaran carries passengers only between Malta and several Sicilian ports.

GUIDES

The National Tourist Organization (tel. 224444/5) can provide you with qualified official guides, who must wear an identification tag issued by the Ministry of Tourism, showing their name, licence number, and a photograph. Your hotel can also find a guide for you. Beware of the many "bargain" tours offered by amateur companies whose driver-guides have little knowledge of their subjects.

Tipping is not included in the price of an excursion.

H

HEALTH and MEDICAL CARE

As in many similar climates in the heat of summer, newcomers to Malta may contract "tourist's tummy," often due to fatigue, too much sun, and a change of diet. Food and drink are quite safe, but be sure fresh fruit and vegetables are washed.

The water is generally safe for drinking, but it can be unpalatable. Do not drink water from fountains. Water in hotels and homes comes straight from the "mains" and is safe. Much mineral water is imported but there is also a good selection of local bottled water.

The local wine can be excellent but the cheapest varieties may have potent laxative effects. If gastrointestinal or other problems last more than a day or two, consult a doctor.

Beware of the sun, which is very powerful in the summer months. Start with a sunscreen or total-block cream at first and build up a tan gradually in small doses. The occasional salt tablet doesn't do any harm when you're perspiring a lot.

There are plenty of insects in country areas, particularly on Gozo and in the hottest part of summer. Several sprays are available in the shops. Tiny, almost invisible flies can leave itching bites; for these, use the insect repellent and itch-remedy creams obtainable at pharmacies. If you have mosquitoes in your room, buy an inexpensive coil called a "moon tiger," which smoulders all night and keeps pests away. Even more effective (and more expensive) is an electric insect repellant.

Insurance. Malta has a reciprocal agreement with the United Kingdom (and certain other countries) providing nearly the same free health care that the British National Health Service offers. But if you come from elsewhere, make sure your health insurance policy covers accident or illness while on holiday.

Treatment. You may not get served in the hospital on silver platters, as the knights of the Order of St. John treated their patients, but medical equipment and treatment are usually of a reasonable standard. General practitioners will be well qualified.

If you need a doctor urgently, your hotel will help you find one; otherwise, the chemist can be of assistance. In an emergency, you can dial 196 on both Malta and Gozo, or:

Malta, St. Luke's Hospital (Gwardamanġa); tel. 241251, 234101.
Gozo, Craig Hospital (Għajn Qatet Street, Victoria); tel. 561600.

Pharmacies. Clearly marked "Chemist" or "Pharmacy," pharmacies are usually open during normal working and shopping hours. Duty pharmacies are listed in the local weekend papers.

HITCHHIKING

It is permitted, though not common. If you do hitchhike, obey the normal common sense rules. Given Malta's cheap and perfectly adequate bus service, you may not find it necessary to hitchhike.

LANGUAGE

You can get along fine if you speak English, since nearly every Maltese has a good command of it, and many speak Italian as well. You'll pick up a few words from signs, as many street names are in *Malti* now. The word for street is *triq*—but the "q" is almost silent. Some of the other consonants are pronounced in apparently exotic ways, but it's worth knowing the rules so that you can say place names correctly. *Xewkija* on Gozo, for example, is pronounced "shoo–KEE-yah". However, the first language here is *Malti* (Maltese), which is both fascinating and quite incomprehensible to most foreigners. The pronunciation is especially difficult. Here is a key to some of the trickier consonants:

ċ	–	like *ch* in *ch*ild
g	–	as in *good*
ġ	–	like *j* in *j*ob
għ	–	silent, unless at the end of a word (*h* as in *h*ello)
h	–	silent, unless at the end of a word (*h* as in *h*ello)
ħ	–	*h*
j	–	like *y* in *y*ear; **aj** like *igh* in h*igh*; **ej** like *ay* in s*ay*
q	–	almost silent—like a very faint *kh*-sound; a bit like cockney glottal stop "ain't i*t*"
x	–	like *sh* in *sh*op
z	–	*ts*
ż	–	*z*

Malta

A Few Everyday Expressions:

	Maltese	pronunciation
good morning	**bonġu**	BON-joo
good evening	**bonswa**	BON-swah
yes	**iva**	EE-vah
no	**le**	leh
please	**jek jogħġbok**	yehekYOJ-bok
thank you	**grazzi**	GRAHT-see
excuse me	**skużi**	SKOO-zee
Where is ...?	**Fejn hu ...?**	fayn oo
right	**lemin**	LEH-meen
left	**xellug**	shehl-LOOG
straight ahead	**dritt il-quddiem**	drit il-KHOOD-dee-ehm
How much?	**Kemm?**	kehm

Ta' means "the place of"

Numbers:

0	**Xejn**	shayn
1	**Wieħed**	WEE-hehd
2	**Tnejn**	tnayn
3	**Tlieta**	TLEE-tah
4	**Erbgħa**	EHR-bah
5	**Ħamsa**	Hum-sah
6	**Sitta**	SIT-tah
7	**Sebgħa**	SEH-bah
8	**Tmienja**	TMEE-ehn-yah
9	**Disgħa**	DIS-sah
10	**Għaxra**	AHSH-rah

Common Town and Site Names:

The Maltese like to hear at least their town names pronounced properly. So here's a list of the main sites mentioned in this book.

Birżebbuġa	beer-zeeb-BOO-jah
Borġ in-Nadur	borj in nah-DOOR
Buġibba	Boo-JIB-ba
Ġgantija	J'GAHN-tee-yah
Għar Dalam	ahr DAH-lam
Għar Ħassan	ahr hahs-SAHN

Għar Lapsi	ahr LAHP-see
Għarb	ahrb
Ħaġar Qim	hah-jahr-khEEM
Marsamxett	mahr-sahm-SHEHTT
Marsaxlokk	mahr-sash-LOKK
Mdina	im-DEE-nah
Mġarr	im-JAHRR
Naxxar	NAHS-shahr
Qala	khAH-lah
Qawra	khOW-rah
Qormi	khOHR-mee
Siġġiewi	SEEJ-jee-eh-wee
Tarxien	TAHR-sheen
Xagħra	SHAH-rah
Xlendi	SHLEHN-dee
Żebbuġ	ZEHB-booj
Żejtun	ZAY-toon

LAUNDRY and DRY CLEANING

There are ample laundry and dry cleaning services on both Malta and
Gozo, and Malta has some self-service launderettes accessible to
tourists during normal business hours. Laundry service takes about
three days, as does dry cleaning. There are express one-day services,
however, and top hotels offer both regular and same-day service.

LOST PROPERTY

Check first where you think you lost the object; the Maltese are, in
general, scrupulously honest about other people's property. If you
can't find the object, check with the nearest police station.

Lost children. Don't let young children out of your sight in crowded places (like the swarming main streets of Valletta). If a child is
missing, go to the police immediately.

M

MAPS

The tourist offices in Valletta and Victoria, Gozo, hand out a very
basic map, which might also be available from your hotel. Otherwise, there's a good choice of maps at bookshops, hotel newsstands,

and the like. The bookshop at the airport has quite a wide selection.

MEETING and GREETING PEOPLE

The islanders tend to have a strict Catholic upbringing, and are usually very polite. They treat each other and strangers with courtesy, and expect the same in return.

Nobody is going to ask you to speak a word of *Malti* (Maltese), but you will get amused and happy smiles if you try out *bonġu* ("good morning") and *bonswa* ("good evening"), *skużi* ("excuse me"), pronounced just like the Italian, and *grazzi* ("thank you"), pronounced almost like the Italian. See also LANGUAGE.

MONEY MATTERS

Currency. The Maltese pound is divided into 100 cents (¢). Within the country, the pound is referred to as *Lira,* plural *Liri* (abbreviated to Lm)

    Notes: Lm 2, 5, 10, 20, and 50.

    Coins: 1¢, 2¢, 5¢, 10¢, 25¢, 50¢ and Lm 1.

Malta's gold and silver proof and brilliant uncirculated coins for collectors can be bought from coin dealers. To take more than just a few souvenir coins out of Malta, you'll need a permit from the Central Bank of Malta.

For currency restrictions, see under CUSTOMS AND ENTRY REGULATIONS.

Banking hours. In summer, hours are 8:00 A.M. to noon, Monday through Friday, (until 11:30 A.M. on Saturdays), 2:30 P.M. to 4:00 P.M. on Fridays; in winter, banks open half an hour later. Some bank branches in main centres have foreign-exchange desks open in the afternoons, from 4:00 P.M. to 7:00 P.M. (3:00 P.M. to 6:00 P.M. in winter). The airport service is open 24 hours. Many banks now have 24-hour automatic banking machines from which users can use bank cards and credit cards to withdraw funds.

On Saturdays, banks will change foreign cash up to the value of Lm 100 for tourists. Many hotels give low rates of exchange for **traveller's cheques,** so it's usually better to go to a bank. You'll need your passport when cashing traveller's cheques. **Credit cards** are widely accepted by major shops, hotels and restaurants in the bigger towns. Usually, the symbols of the cards accepted are on display. In shops, pay with Maltese currency or credit cards, unless they are advertising a special high rate for your foreign currency.

Prices are reasonable when compared with the big continental cities. Food is inexpensive. Handicrafts (weaving, lace, knitting, pottery, glass, etc.) are good buys (see Shopping, page 87). Prices are usually fixed, but you can try your bargaining skills at market stalls, street stands and some smaller jewellers selling souvenirs. Some prices are listed on page 122 as a guide.

NEWSPAPERS and MAGAZINES

All the British dailies and the *International Herald Tribune* are usually available in the afternoon of the day of publication (the next day on Gozo) at most newsstands. There is one English-language daily published in Malta, *The Times*, and two English-language weekly papers, *The Sunday Times* and *The Malta Independent*.

The small fortnightly *What's On* guide gives a vast amount of information on everything from restaurants and cinemas to tips for the tourist.

OPENING HOURS

Everything closes up for a few hours around lunchtime. The summer heat can be unbearable; so do as the locals do—relax until the cool of late afternoon.

Hours of opening vary widely according to the establishment, whether government or private, the day of the week, and the time of year. The following is an indication of the general rules. (See also under POST OFFICES and MONEY MATTERS.)

Government offices. Winter (1 October to 15 June): 7:45 A.M. to 12:30 P.M. and 1:15 P.M. to 5:15 P.M., Monday through Friday. Summer: 7.30 A.M. to 1.30 P.M., Monday through Friday.

Offices and Businesses. 8:30 A.M. or 9:00 A.M. to 1:00 P.M. or 1:30 P.M. and 2:30 P.M. to 5:30 P.M. or 6:00 P.M., Monday through Friday. A few operate on Saturday mornings. Most head or managing offices follow Government schedules.

Shopping hours are generally from 9:00 A.M. to 7:00 P.M. with a one- to three-hour break for lunch (usually closer to three), Monday through Saturday. Some establishments remain open during lunch, and some stay open until 8:00 P.M. on Saturdays.

The open-air market in Merchants Street, Valletta, operates until about noon, Monday through Saturday. On Sundays, a much larger morning market attracts crowds to St. James Ditch just outside the walls of Valletta, a stone's throw from the bus terminus.

Museums. Most museums and sites are state-run and have fairly uniform hours. Winter (1 October to 15 June): 8:15 A.M. to 5:00 P.M., Monday through Saturday; 8:15 A.M. to 4:15 P.M. on Sunday. Summer: 8:15 A.M. to 1:30 A.M. but 8:30 A.M. to 5:00 P.M., Monday, Wednesday, Friday. Closed on public holidays. In Gozo, government museums are open 8:30 A.M. to 4:30 P.M., Monday through Saturday in winter; 8:30 A.M. to 6:30 P.M. or 7:00 P.M. in summer; 8:30 A.M. to 3:00 P.M. on Sundays all year round. At the Hypogeum, Paola, visitor numbers are restricted: you may have to wait to join a group to go in. (The site is still closed.)

Mdina Cathedral Museum. 9:00 A.M. to 1:00 P.M. and 1:30 P.M. to 4:30 P.M. Closed on Sunday and on public holidays.

Manoel Theatre. Tours 10:45 A.M. and 11:30 A.M., Monday through Friday; 11:30 A.M., Saturday. Closed on Sunday and on public holidays.

National War Museum, Fort St. Elmo. Same times as for state museums.

War Rooms, Lascaris Bastion. 9:30 A.M. to 4:30 P.M., Monday through Friday; 9:30 A.M. to 1:00 P.M. on weekends and on public holidays.

St. John's Co-Cathedral and Museum. 9:30 A.M. to 12:55 P.M. and 1:30 P.M. to 4:55 P.M., Monday through Friday; 9:30 A.M. to 12:55 P.M., Saturday. Closed on Sunday and on public holidays (except for religious functions).

The Malta Experience, Mediterranean Conference Centre. Shows every hour on the hour 11:00 A.M. to 4:00 P.M., Monday through Friday; 11:00 A.M., noon, and 1:00 P.M., on weekends and public holidays.

Gozo Heritage, Mġarr Road. 9:00 A.M. to 5:15 P.M., Monday through Saturday; by appointment on Sunday.

The Mdina Experience, 7 Mesquita Street. Hourly shows 11:00 A.M. to 4:00 P.M., Monday through Friday; 11:00 A.M. through 2:00 P.M., Saturday. Closed on Sunday and on public holidays.

PHOTOGRAPHY

There are plenty of subjects to appeal to the amateur or professional—spectacular views where cliffs of pastel-coloured rock tumble into the dark blue or turquoise sea, colourful fishing boats, craftspeople at work, the gold of sunset on ancient walls, and the special challenge of underwater photography. The deep shadows of alleyways and the fierce light of midday at prehistoric sites are a severe test to your photographic skills.

Most well-known film brands are available, but not everywhere. Valletta has several good photography shops. You may have trouble buying 35-mm black and white film or especially fast film, but major brands of colour print and transparency film are easy to find.

Fast black-and-white development is rare. Colour print film is processed the same day on weekdays. There is also a one-hour service available.

The airport's X–ray machine does not spoil normal film, but for safety's sake, put it in a bag to be checked separately.

Video tape is readily available. Remember, though, that videotape or pre-made videos you buy on Malta may not be compatible with your VCR equipment back home; check before you buy.

POLICE

Most towns have a police station, clearly marked. Some stations are not manned around the clock. All police officers, whether watching traffic or helping a tourist find the way, are dressed in casual blue cotton uniforms in summer, black uniforms in winter, with visored hats. Don't hesitate to approach them: they are helpful and friendly.

Always contact the police immediately in case of a car accident (see under DRIVING). In an emergency, call the police on 191.

POST OFFICES

The postal service is generally quite efficient in Malta. The General Post Office at Auberge d'Italie in Merchants Street, Valletta keeps the following hours:

Summer: (16 June to 30 September): 7:30 A.M. to 6:00 P.M., Monday through Saturday.

Winter: 8:00 A.M. to 6:30 P.M., Monday through Saturday.

Branch post offices are open 7:30 A.M. to 12:45 P.M., Monday through Saturday all year round.

The main branch post office on Gozo is at 129 Republic (Racecourse) Street, Victoria. Hours are the same as Malta's.

Stamps may also be bought at most hotels, some tobacconists and some shops that sell postcards. Mailboxes are painted red.

Poste Restante (general delivery). If you wish to have your mail sent to you c/o Poste Restante, you should write ahead of time to warn the post office (address the letter to the Postmaster General, General Post Office, Valletta, Malta).When going to collect your mail, you will need proof of identity, or if you are sending someone to collect it for you, you will need to give them written authorization.

Telegrams. You can send telegrams from Telemalta in South Street, Valletta, 8:00 A.M. to 6:30 P.M., Monday through Saturday (except holidays), from Luqa Airport every day 7:00 A.M. to 7:00 P.M. or from the Main Telegraph Office (open 24 hours a day), St. George's Road, St. Julian's.

There is no local telegram service (and little point in sending telegrams to the UK, where they are only telephoned to the recipient and later delivered with the mail).

Telex. Your hotel may have a telex that you can use. Public telex facilities are available in South Street, Valletta, and at Luqa Airport, 9:00 A.M. to 5:30 P.M., Monday through Saturday (except holidays), and at St. George's Road Main Telegraph Office at the same hours from Monday through Friday (except holidays).

Fax. Facsimile transmission services are available at Telemalta main offices in Valletta, Sliema, St. Julian's and Victoria (Gozo). Your hotel may also offer this service.

PRICES

To give you an idea of what to expect, here is a list of average prices in Malta Liri (Lm). They can only be approximate, especially where competing prices prevail (e.g., car hire, souvenirs, water sports).

Accommodation. Per person, per night, with breakfast. 5-star Lm 50, 4-star Lm 19, 3-star Lm 14, 2-star Lm 10, 1-star Lm 8. Aparthotels and similar accomodations: Lm 10–23 per apartment (double bed), depending on quality and facilities. Guesthouses: Lm 6–10.

Airport transfer. Taxi to Valletta, meter fare Lm 4.50 (plus 15% VAT).

Car hire. Officially the daily tariff is Lm 7 irrespective of make of car but excluding petrol (gasoline). Last minute bookings in summer may exceed this: out-of-season rates and advance reservations made before arrival can be less. 15% VAT will be added.

Ferry to Gozo. From Ċirkewwa to Mġarr, return, adults Lm 1.50, children 50¢, Lm 3.50 per car. Fares are the same from Sa Maison Pier, Pietà.

Food and drinks. Set meal (tourist menu) in medium-priced restaurant Lm 2.75–3.50, bottle of local wine from Lm 1.20, soft drinks 23¢, coffee 30¢, beer 35¢ (plus 10% VAT on food; 15% on drinks).

Guides. Half-day tour Lm 15, full day (8 hrs.) Lm 20. Full-day tour must be topped with a free lunch for the guide or Lm 2 as an allowance for lunch.

Shopping. Beef, fresh from Lm 3 per kilogram (2 pounds), frozen from Lm 1.20 per kilogram (2 pounds), chicken (frozen) Lm 1 per kilogram (2 pounds), potatoes 15¢ per kilogram (2 pounds), loaf of bread 13¢ for 750 grams (1 pound 8 ounces), butter 20¢ for 227 grams (8 ounces), milk 12¢ per bottle, local wine 30¢–Lm 1.30 per bottle, whisky/gin Lm 5.50–6 per bottle.

Souvenirs. Set of three Maltese lace placemats Lm 3.95–8.50, silver cufflinks with Maltese cross Lm 5–6, gold filigree brooch Lm 20, silver filigree brooch Lm 4–8.

Water sports. *Canoe* Lm 1.75 per hour, *sailing dinghy* Lm 5–10 for two hours, *windsurfer* Lm 4 per hour, *jet-bike* Lm 10 for 15 minutes, *water-skiing* Lm 15 for 20-minute lesson, *scuba diving* Lm 10–12 per dive, Lm 44 for 4 dives.

PUBLIC HOLIDAYS

These are the official civic and religious holidays when banks, offices, and shops are closed. Not listed are the numerous *festi* on various weekends in different towns, though then shops usually remain open on Saturdays.

1 January	New Year's Day
10 February	St. Paul's Shipwreck
19 March	St. Joseph's Day
31 March	Freedom Day
1 May	May Day or Workers' Day
7 June	Commemoration of 7 June 1919
29 June	St. Peter and St. Paul
15 August	Feast of the Assumption
8 September	Our Lady of Victories
21 September	Independence Day
8 December	Immaculate Conception
13 December	Republic Day
25 December	Christmas Day
Moveable date	Good Friday

PUBLIC TRANSPORT (See also CAR HIRE)

Bus services. All towns and many villages are linked up by low-cost, regular, and efficient services, though in summer the buses get rather hot and crowded. Pay your fare to the driver. In Valletta, buses for all parts of the island leave from the Triton Fountain just outside City Gate. In Victoria, Gozo, the terminal is in Main Gate Street. Destinations are indicated by numbers on the bus, and you can find out which number goes where from boards at the station, or by asking at your hotel desk, the Tourist Office, or a bus driver. Buses are orange and yellow (Malta) or red and light grey (Gozo).

Taxis. They are white, are clearly marked "Taxi" and have red number plates. All have meters, and drivers will give you an estimate of the cost of a journey in advance. A small tip (about 10%) is expected, especially when the driver has been helpful in carrying your luggage. Cabs are readily available at the airport, as well as at main hotels, around tourist centres, and at the ferry docks. Hotel receptionists will order taxis for you.

Ferries. Apart from a helicopter link, the only way to get to Gozo is by boat. Sailings between Malta and Gozo are frequent, although bad weather may interrupt the service.

One passenger and car ferry leaves from Sa Maison Pier in Pietà Creek, Floriana, for the main Gozo harbour, Mġarr, a trip of 1 hour 15 minutes, leaving at approximately 9:30 A.M., Monday through Friday, returning at 5:00 P.M. It has a large, air-conditioned passenger lounge and a cafeteria.

Another car and passenger ferry service runs from Cirkewwa in northwest Malta to Mġarr several times a day. It's only a 30-minute trip, but if you start from Valletta or the airport, you have to drive to the other end of the island first. The service operates every half hour in winter and on shuttle service in July and August (when there are sailings during the night).

For further information telephone 243964 (Sa Maison), 571884 (Ċirkewwa), 556114 (Mġarr) or 556016 (recorded information).

On Comino, the island's sole hotel runs a regular boat service to Marfa (on Malta) and Gozo at least six times a day during the summer season; telephone 573464/529821 for further details.

In addition, travel agencies and cruise companies operate Comino cruises daily. Also in summer, fast hydrofoil services operate to Gozo from Sliema and Buġibba.

Horse-drawn cabs. First introduced in the 1850s, the *karrozzin,* or horse-drawn cab, has now become simply a leisurely way of visiting Valletta, Mdina, and Sliema. For a rate definitely to be negotiated in advance, you can tour the main sights of the towns for an hour or so. Pick up a cab at the Customs House or at Great Siege Square in Valletta; in Sliema, try at the Promenade in front of the Hotel Preluna; and in Mdina, beside Bastion Square or Mdina Gate.

Water-taxis. Somewhat reminiscent of a gondola, the brightly painted *dgħajsa* (pronounced "DIGH-sa"), or water-taxi, plies Malta's main harbours. *Dgħajjes* can be hired (at rates to be negotiated) at the Customs House in Valletta and on the waterfronts at Senglea and Vittoriosa.

R

RADIO and TV
Several local radio stations transmit in English; Smash Radio (104.6

FM) 24 hours non-stop music, Radio Calypso (102.3 FM), Bay Radio (102.6 FM), Island Sound (101.8 FM).

On shortwave bands, reception of the BBC World Service is clear. Voice of America programmes are also easily picked up.

Television Malta transmits in Maltese and English, including both British and American features, and is tuned in to CNN overnight. Most TV sets are also tuned to receive the Italian national television networks and several Sicilian local stations.

RELIGIOUS SERVICES

Malta is almost 100 percent Catholic. Most services are in Maltese. For non-Maltese Roman Catholics, St. Barbara Church on Republic Street, Valletta, celebrates mass in French, German and English at various times. Several other denominations also have churches in Malta; see the weekend newspapers or *What's On* guide, or check with your high commission, embassy or consulate.

T

TELEPHONE

Public telephone boxes are found in many streets and squares; in Valletta and Mdina the traditional red English booths still exist. Phones are card-operated (telecards can be purchased at TeleMalta offices or from authorized dealers) and phone booths for overseas calls are clearly marked. Information in the telephone directory is in Maltese and English. For local calls, you can usually dial direct from your hotel room or by asking the operator for a line. Some hotels allow nonguests to use their lobby phones.

Overseas calls can be dialled direct to many countries, using the prefix **00** followed by the destination code. For information, dial **194** to get the overseas telephone exchange. Hotels are authorized to add an extra charge for calls placed.

For the directory enquiry service dial **190.**

The country code for Malta when dialling from elsewhere is **356.**

TIME DIFFERENCES

Malta uses Central European Time (GMT + 1) and in summer (31 March until the third Sunday in September) clocks are put one hour ahead (= GMT + 2). Dial 195 for a time check.

Summer chart:

New York	London	**Valletta**	Jo'burg	Sydney	Auckland
6:00 A.M.	11:00 A.M.	**noon**	noon	8:00 P.M.	10:00 P.M.

TIPPING

A service charge is sometimes included in restaurant bills, but in any case it is customary to leave a small tip as well. The chart below gives some suggestions as to how much to leave.

Porter, per bag	25¢ to 50¢
Hotel maid, per week	Lm 1
Waiter	10%
Lavatory attendant	10¢
Taxi driver	10%
Hairdresser/Barber	10 to 15%

TOILETS

There are few public conveniences and these are only in the larger towns. The signs differentiating men's and women's toilets are very subtle—sometimes you have to ask. If you see an attendant, you may give him or her a few cents. "Keep this place clean," cautions one sign in a Valletta convenience. "Legal action will be taken." Cafés and bars usually have facilities you can use.

TOURIST INFORMATION OFFICES

There is an Air Malta information desk at the airport, where they can advise about hotels and give other information.

The office to contact for detailed brochures on hotels, self-catering flats, etc. is the National Tourist Organization at:

280 Republic Street, Valletta; tel. 224444/225048.

There is also a tourist information office at: 1, City Gate Arcade, Valletta; tel. 237747 and others at main holiday centres, where the staff also give brochures and maps.

In Gozo, go to the Tourist Information Office at Mġarr Harbour, near the ferry landing pier (tel. 553343) or in Palm Street, Victoria (tel. 558106).

Tourist organizations and information for Malta abroad:
United Kingdom: Malta National Tourist Office, Malta House,

Malta

36/38 Piccadilly Street, London W1V OPP; tel. (171) 292 4900.

USA and Canada: Malta National Tourist Office, Empire State Building, 350 Fifth Avenue, Suite 4412, New York, NY 10118; tel. (212) 695-9520 or:

Embassy of Malta, 2017 Connecticut Avenue NW, Washington DC 20008; tel. (202) 462-3611/2.

WEIGHTS and MEASURES

Length

Weight

Temperature

YOUTH HOSTELS

There are several youth hostels in Malta and one in Gozo. For information, contact the Malta Youth Hostels Association:

17 Tal-Borg Street, Paola; tel. 693957

A SELECTION
OF HOTELS
AND RESTAURANTS

Recommended Hotels

Hotel prices have risen in recent years, but they are still quite reasonable by the standards of many Mediterranean destinations. Most hotels are concentrated in a few areas, alongside holiday apartments, some time-shares, and a few villas. Since distances are short, everywhere on Malta is easily accessible— and even more so on Gozo.

Some of the hotels that cater for groups may be full from May to October, and the season seems to be getting longer. A few hotels close for the mid-winter months. If you are buying a package holiday, remember that some hotels play safe and serve a rather dull and bland diet. If you pay for halfboard rather than full board, you'll be free to try the wide variety of other eating places.

Our Berlitz choices, listed alphabetically, area by area, are made with the help of experienced travellers and island residents, taking account of quality, location, price, and character. The following selection is not meant to be exclusive: we don't have space for all the good places, and new ones are opening up all the time.

As a basic guide, we have used the symbols below to indicate the price for a double room with bath or shower, including breakfast. Winter prices are often significantly less. (Note that Maltese hotels usually quote a rate *per person*.) The telephone country code for Malta is 356.

✪✪✪	above Lm 25
✪✪	Lm 15–25
✪	below Lm 15

VALLETTA AREA AND THE SOUTHEAST

Alfonso ✪✪ *Triq il Qaghliet, St. Julian's Bay; Tel. 330053; Fax 344880.* Charming hotel near nightclubs, restaurants, discos, and the International Casino de Malte in St. Julian's. Panoramic views.

Castille ✪✪ *Castille Square, Valletta; Tel. 243677; Fax 243677.* Close to City Gate and Upper Barrakka Gardens, in a restored 16th/17th-century house. Rooftop terrace.

Fortina ✪✪ *Tigne Sea Front, Sliema; Tel. 343380; Fax 332004.* Modern block with fine views facing south near Dragut Point. Pools, water sports, fitness facilities, tennis. Entertainment.

Holiday Inn Crowne Plaza ✪✪✪ *Tigne Street, Sliema; Tel. 341173/341183; Fax 311292.* Stunning views of Marsamxett Harbour from this luxury hotel. Three restaurants, gym, sauna, tennis courts, squash, indoor and outdoor pools, piano bar. 182 rooms all with good facilities.

Imperial ✪✪ *1 Rudolphe Street, Sliema; Tel. 344787; Fax 336471.* Comfortable hotel in an older part of Sliema, just a short walk from the waterfront. Sundeck and pool.

Jerma Palace ✪✪✪ *Dawret it-Tori, Marsaskala; Tel. 823222; Fax 829485.* Large and spectacular resort hotel on a rocky point near the fishing harbour of Marsaskala. Bars, restaurant, and nightclub. Swimming pools, water sports, and a variety of fitness facilities.

Kennedy Court ✪✪ *166 The Strand, Sliema; Tel. 345480; Fax 341871.* South/harbour-facing bright and modern hotel. Swimming pool, rooftop terrace, health and fitness facilities.

Marina ✪✪ *Tigne Sea Front, Sliema; Tel. 336461; Fax 330650.* Tall, functional block facing harbour. Rooftop terrace.

Milano Due ✪ *113 The Strand, Gzira, near Sliema; Tel. 345040/3; Fax 345045.* Bright, modern harbourside block. Simple rooms. Delightful rooftop restaurant.

Phoenicia Hotel ✪✪✪ *The Mall, Floriana; Tel. 225241; Fax 235254.* Centrally situated, this grand hotel retains its elegant style and high quality. Excellent service, but expensive.

Preluna Towers ✪✪✪ *124 Tower Road, Sliema; Tel. 334001/9; Fax 342292.* Modern block facing north with stunning views. Pools, night entertainment.

ST. PAUL'S BAY AND THE NORTH

Carolina ✪ *St. Anthony Street, Bugibba; Tel. 571536/4; Fax 573602.* Pleasant atmosphere. Swimming pools, nightclub, disabled facilities. 53 rooms.

Golden Sands ✪✪✪ *Golden Bay, Ghajn Tuffieha; Tel. 573961/3; Fax 580875.* Big resort hotel on the cliff above the beautiful sandy bay. Swimming pools, water sports, diving, tennis, entertainment.

Liliana ✪✪ *Tirq ic-Centurjun, Bugibba; Tel. 572330; Fax 581270.* 80 rooms in pleasant hotel. Close to Roosendaal complex with swimming pool which guests staying at the Liliana can use without charge.

New Dolmen ✪✪✪ *(midway between Bugibba and Qwara), Promenade, Bugibba; Tel. 581510/8; Fax 581532.* Very large resort hotel and sports complex on St. Paul's Bay. Pools, tennis, squash, water sports, fitness facilities, entertainment. Neolithic site within gardens. Conference centre.

Qawra Palace ✪✪ *Qawra Coast Road, Qawra; Tel. 580131/2; Fax 580662.* Big, modern resort hotel opposite rocky shore. Pools, water sports, fitness facilities.

Ramla Bay ✪✪✪ *Ramla Bay, Marfa; Tel. 573521/3; Fax 575931.* At the northern tip of Malta, by its own small, private, sandy beach and rocky shore. Good facilities with pools, water sports, tennis, and entertainment.

Suncrest ✪✪✪ *Qawra Coast Road, Qawra; Tel. 577101; Fax 575478.* 413 twin rooms, each with balcony and most with good sea views. Outdoor pools, five restaurants, nightclub, cocktails, water sports centre, and floodlit tennis courts.

RABAT/MDINA AND THE SOUTHWEST

Corinthia Palace ✪✪✪ *De Paule Avenue, Attard; Tel. 440301/9; Fax 465713.* Luxury hotel situated next to San Anton gardens. Offers a high standard of comfort and service; facilities include a health and fitness centre.

Grand Hotel Verdala ✪✪✪ *Inguanez Street, Rabat; Tel. 451700/7; Fax 451708.* Hilltop retreat convenient to Mdina, with comfortable, traditional rooms. Gardens, pools, and a disco.

GOZO AND COMINO

Atlantis ✪ *Qolla Street, Marsalforn, Gozo; Tel. 554685; Fax 555661.* Small, modern block a couple of minutes' walk from the bay.

Calypso ✪✪ *Marsalforn, Gozo; Tel. 562000; Fax 562012.* Big, modern, functional block by the harbour. Pool, water sports, diving, tennis, squash. Disco and Chinese restaurant.

Comino ✪✪✪ *Island of Comino; Tel. 529821/9; Fax 529826.* Self-contained resort with extensive range of facilities; bungalows available. Pools, water sports, diving, tennis courts, disco.

Cornucopia ✪✪ *10 Gnien Imrik Street, Xaghra, Gozo; Tel. 556486; Fax 552910.* Converted farmhouse just outside the little hilltop town, with attractive, modern rooms in extensions around the gardens and pools.

Serena ✪ *Upper St. Simon Street, Xlendi, Gozo; Tel. 553719; Fax 557452.* Apartment hotel situated on a cliff above the inlet, with pleasant, bright rooms. Rooftop pool and terrace. Water sports.

Ta' Ċenċ ✪✪✪ *Sannat, Gozo; Tel. 561522/5; Fax 558199.* Luxury accommodation with 82 rooms. Facilities include two outdoor pools, indoor heated pool and health centre.

Recommended Restaurants

To give a rough guide to the price of a three-course meal with wine, restaurants are classified as follows:

✪✪✪	above Lm12
✪✪	Lm 8–12
✪	below 8 Lm

You can, of course, eat a filling plate of pasta or a local dish for very much less, and some medium-priced restaurants offer a "tourist menu" for Lm 2.50–3.50. Service is normally included in restaurant prices; 10% VAT is charged on food and 15% on drinks. A tip of 10–15% is expected for good service.

Unless otherwise stated, the restaurants listed below are open daily for lunch and dinner. We do not attempt to list beach cafés, fast-food outlets and bars serving food, good value though they may be. They number in their hundreds.

VALLETTA AREA AND THE SOUTHEAST

Beluga ✪✪ *Ramla Road, Marsaskala; Tel. 829452.* Fish and international menu in an elegant setting by the sea.

Bologna ✪✪ *59 Republic Street, Valletta; Tel. 246149.* City-centre setting. Italian cuisine. Closed Sundays and public holidays.

Bouzouki ✪✪ *Spinola Road, St. Julian's; Tel. 317127.* Greek cuisine served in an informal setting.

Cotton Club ✪✪ *Dragonara Road, Paceville, St. Julian's; Tel. 319347.* Italian cuisine. Upstairs in modern block, next to its own disco.

Fisherman's Rest ✪✪ *St. Thomas Bay, Zejtun; Tel. 822049.* Fish and international cuisine, in an informal, waterside setting. Closed Mondays.

Giannini ✪✪✪ *23 Windmill Street, Valletta; Tel. 237121/236575.* Elegant setting with breathtaking views of Marsamxett harbour. Maltese–Italian cuisine.

Il'Ghonella ✪✪ *Spinola Palace, St. Julian's; Tel. 341027.* Set in cellars of old palace. International and Italian menu. Closed Tuesdays.

Il-Parapett ✪ *St. George's Road, St. Julian's; Tel. 333394.* Italian and Maltese dishes and snacks. Cheerful and informal atmosphere.

La Veneziana ✪ *29-30 Melita Street, Valletta; Tel. 222513.* Snacks and pizzas. Informal café, convenient for city centre.

Mangal ✪✪ *Tigne Sea Front, Sliema; Tel. 341046/342976.* In Fortina Hotel on waterfront. Authentic Turkish cuisine and grills. Closed lunchtime July and August.

San Giuliano ✪✪✪ *Spinola Bay, St. Julian's; Tel. 332000.* Elegantly situated right over the harbour. Wide range of Italian dishes.

Skuna II ✪✪ *4 Duncan Street, Marsaxlokk; Tel. 871317.* Informal restaurant near harbour. Fish specialities. Closed Tuesdays and public holidays.

Trattoria Palazz ✪ *43 Old Theatre Street, Valletta; Tel. 226611.* Fine selection of pasta and meat dishes. Clean, elegant, good service. Closed Sundays and public holidays.

ST. PAUL'S BAY AND THE NORTH

Arches ✪✪✪ *113 Main Street, Mellieha; Tel. 573436/520533.* Widely known for its inventive French and international cuisine. Closed lunchtime and Sundays.

Cross Keys ✪ *Cross Square, Mellieha; Tel. 572587.* Lively, with international dishes and snacks. Open evenings only.

Gillieru ✪✪✪ *Church Street, St. Paul's Bay; Tel. 573480/573269.* Large harbourside restaurant serving a variety of fish and international dishes.

It-Tokk ✪✪ *Qawra Coast, Qawra; Tel. 577101.* In the Suncrest Hotel. Specializing in Maltese dishes, including antipasti served on a real luzzu fishing boat.

Portobello ✪✪ *St. Luke Street, Bugibba; Tel. 571661.* Pasta and fish dishes, international cuisine. Meals served on terrace over the water.

Savini ✪✪ *Qawra Road, Salina Bay; Tel. 576927.* Wide range of Italian cuisine in old house with rooftop terrace. Closed Sundays.

Ta' Cassia ✪✪ *Qawra Road, Salina Bay; Tel. 571435.* In old farmhouse. Maltese, pasta, and fish dishes. Evenings only.

RABAT/MDINA AND THE SOUTHWEST

Bacchus ✪✪ *Inguanez Alley, Mdina; Tel. 454981.* International, Italian, and Maltese dishes in the cellars of an attractive old mansion.

Cosmana Navarra ✪✪ *28 St. Paul Street, Rabat; Tel. 450638.* Modern cuisine in a charming old house. Closed on Sundays and public holidays.

Medina ✪✪✪ *7 Holy Cross Street, Mdina; Tel. 454004.* Set in fine old house, with courtyard dining in summer. French, international, and Maltese menu. Closed Sundays and public holidays.

GOZO

Auberge Ta' Frenc ✪✪✪ *Marsalforn Road, between Victoria and Marsalforn, Gozo; Tel. 553888.* Old farmhouse, attractively extended. French and international cuisine. Closed Mondays, and lunchtime Fridays and Sundays lunchtime.

Il Castello (Amand's Bistro & Restaurant) ✪✪ *Qbajjar Bay, Marsalforn, Gozo; Tel. 551197/555179.* French and international cuisine served in a historical castle (1690–1720) built by Grand Master Perellos under the Knights of St. John. The restaurant has outdoor tables, a non-smoking section, and access for the disabled. It is open everyday from 10:30 a.m. to 3:00 p.m. and 7:00 p.m. to 11:00 p.m.

Forchetta ✪✪ *Qolla Street, Marsalforn, Gozo; Tel. 551568.* Cheerful, informal restaurant. Italian cuisine and snacks.